How to Day Trade Penny Stocks for Beginners

Find Out How You Can Trade For a Living Using Unique Trading Psychology, Expert Tools and Tactics, and Winning Strategies.

Bill Sykes

Timothy Gibbs

© **Copyright 2019 - All rights reserved.**

The content contained within this book may not be reproduced, duplicated, or transmitted without direct written permission from the author or the publisher.

Under no circumstances will any blame or legal responsibility be held against the publisher, or author, for any damages, reparation, or monetary loss due to the information contained within this book. Either directly or indirectly.

Legal Notice:

This book is copyright protected. This book is only for personal use. You cannot amend, distribute, sell, use, quote or paraphrase any part, or the content within this book, without the consent of the author or publisher.

Disclaimer Notice:

Please note the information contained within this document is for educational and entertainment purposes only. All effort has been executed to present accurate, up to date, and reliable, complete information. No warranties of any kind are declared or implied. Readers acknowledge that the author is not engaging in the rendering of legal, financial, medical, or professional advice. The content within this book has been derived from various sources. Please consult a licensed professional before attempting any techniques outlined in this book.

By reading this document, the reader agrees that under no circumstances is the author responsible for any losses, direct or indirect, which are incurred as a result of the use of the information contained within this document, including, but not limited to, — errors, omissions, or inaccuracies.

Table of Contents

Introduction

Chapter 1: Get Familiar with Stocks

Why Do Companies Sell Stock?
The stock market

Chapter 2: Investing Versus Trading

Being an Investor

Being a Trader

Chapter 3: The Basics of Penny Stocks

Traditional Markets

Why Penny Stocks Are So Profitable

Shortcomings of Penny Stocks

The Pump and Dump Scheme

Chapter 4: Personality Traits of a Successful Penny Stock Investor

Do you enjoy actively managing and monitoring your portfolio?

Will you be satisfied with a modest return?

Can you tell when someone's lying to you?

Do you cope well with risk?

Are you okay with letting it ride?

Chapter 5: Pink Sheets

Who Can Be Pink Sheet-Listed?

The Difference between Pink Sheets and OTCBB

The Benefits of Pink Sheets

Risks Associated with Pink Sheets

The Workings of the Pink Sheet Tier System

Chapter 6: Getting Started

Research

Choose a Broker to set up an Online Brokerage Account

Buy

Sell

How to open up an Account

Starting with Paper Trading

Transitioning to Investing with Real Money

Choosing a Broker
Overall
Low Commissions
Platforms
Ending Notes

How to Select Penny Stocks
Share Price
Dilution

How to Seek out the Winners

How to Find a Penny Stock Before It Spikes

The Payoff Potential in Penny Stocks

Chapter 7: Strategies

1. Examine the waves
2. Block out others
3. Don't expect too much
4. Have a plan
5. Don't let your emotions get in the way
6. Keep a journal

Dollar Cost Averaging (DCA)

Reverse Mergers

Stop-Loss Orders

Position Sizing

When to Take and When to Sell a Profit

Moving Averages (MA)

Chapter 8: Risk Management

The Risks Associated with Penny Stocks

10 Ways to Protect Yourself and Prepare for Financial Freedom

Chapter 9: Identifying Good Companies

Look for Companies Matching a Strong Angle with Financial Competence

The company provides relentless value at every interaction point.
The company stands out from the crowd.
The company cultivates focus in its branding.
The company communicates well.
The company cultivates its own distinct and consistent style.

The Penny Stock Branding Advantage

Perform Technical and Fundamental Analyses

before Buying

The Typical Penny Stock

How and When to Cash In

Chapter 10: Metrics

Liquidity Ratios

Growth Rates

The Price-to-Earnings Ratio

When the Penny Stock Doesn't Have Earnings

Where Do I Find All These Ratios?

Chapter 11: Technical Analysis

The Positives of Technical Analysis

The Negatives of Technical Analysis

Chapter 12: Working as a Professional

Factors to Stay Aware of When Mastering Penny Stocks

How to Increase Your Effectiveness and Skill in Penny Stocks

Protection from the Downfalls of Investing in Penny Stocks

A Method for Getting Great at Investing in Penny Stocks

Chapter 13: Don't Get Scammed

Tools and Strategies Used In Penny Stock Scams

Why People Become Interested in Penny

Stocks

Considerations in Buying a Penny Stock

Types of Penny Stock Scams

Avoiding Scams

Chapter 14: Tips and Tricks

Chapter 15: How to Find the Right Help

Screen Your Advice and Advisors

Look for a Verifiable Track Record

Conclusion

References

Introduction

Congratulations on downloading your personal copy of *Penny Stocks for Beginners: A Complete Guide to Investing in Penny Stocks, Day Trading, Passive Income, and Massive Wealth.* Thank you for doing so.

In this book, we're going to spend some time learning about penny stocks and why they are among the best options to consider when deciding to get involved in investing. While there are many choices within the world of investing, penny stocks can be an interesting one to decide upon and one that has the possibility of bringing in a lot of profit. This book contains everything you need to know about penny stocks so that you can learn how to start using this investment tool for your own benefit.

First, we will start with some of the basics concerning penny stocks and how they are different from other stocks that are available. We will also discuss the two main options for penny stocks - namely the pink sheets and the Over-the-Counter Bulletins. Once you've had a chance to learn about these basics, we will delve deep into the topic of penny stock investing. We'll touch on how to get into the game and find a good broker before moving on to some of the top strategies you can implement to put your money to work and find out which penny stocks will work best for you. The book will conclude with some basic tips that can help you really see results, even as a beginner.

Investing in penny stocks is a great way to open up your portfolio so that your money can grow more than ever before. However, it does take some time and effort in order to learn this method and make it work well for you. This guidebook is going to give you the tips that you need to get started creating a good income with penny stocks.

There are plenty of books on this subject available on the market, so thank you again for choosing this one. Please enjoy!

Chapter 1: Get Familiar with Stocks

Have you thought about using any passive income sources? Do you have a desire to be part of a profitable investment? If so, you should definitely consider investing in the stock market. Though investing in stocks is a profitable venture, it is a difficult one. You will be required to learn several things in regard to stock investments before you can begin buying the quoted shares in the stock exchange market. Do not make the mistake of buying stocks before understanding the basics; you will regret it in the long run.

To put it simply, one share of stocks is the representation of a partial claim that the owner has towards the earnings and assets of the issuing company. If the number of shares available in the market is higher, then it means a single share will have less worth. If one has a higher number of shares for a particular company, then that individual has greater control over the company. Any owner of stock in a particular company is regarded as a shareholder, implying that they own a portion of the profits of the company (Hayes, 2013). Such portions are normally called dividends. The payment of dividends is made on predetermined points of any particular year. If you have shares of a specific company, you may have voting rights regarding the decisions of the company, in which case you can influence its future progress.

You should note that owning shares of a particular company does not give you an active say in the daily operations of the company. Owning shares provides you with entitlement to a profit share and voting shares. During the annual shareholder meeting, you have the possibility to vote for the members who constitute the board of directors. This is the moment where you have the chance to express your satisfaction or dissatisfaction towards the current setup of the company or how it's run.

When you decide to invest in the stock market, it is paramount that you understand the risk. Be considerate of the companies you resolve to invest in, and identify whether they pay out dividends; not all companies do so, and it's not a guarantee that one that paid out dividends previously will continue doing it. This is because, when talking about the stock market, profits are never 100 percent guaranteed. It is impossible to count on continuous stock appreciation in generating more value. There will be reasons that may contribute to the slipping of a given stock. It's also possible that the company could declare bankruptcy.

Don't consider the risk with negative thoughts, though; consider it as a tool that can help you evaluate the potential of a given stock. If a particular stock presents a greater risk, then the possibility of reward is high if it moves in the direction you want it to. If you carefully take the time to understand the risk, you will generate a return that's higher than the standard 7 percent promised by many investments; you may even reach a profit of 12 percent.

Why Do Companies Sell Stock?

A company sells stock when it needs to raise money. It can also do this by borrowing funds from a bank or another source (Metcalf, 2019). However, if its owners choose to sell stock, there are no repayment plans you'll face in the future.

There are a few different ways to sell stock. If a company's owners want to control who is offered a piece of the pie, they sell stock through "private placement," which allows the management to choose to whom the stock is offered.

Chances are that if you've purchased stock or plan to do so in the future, you've done so through a public offering. Companies initiate public offerings, as was noted, in order to raise money. They may need money for a variety of reasons, including expansion or any other kind of further growth, or to pay back owners or investors who had a hand in starting the company.

Companies set up an initial public offering (IPO), which is the first offering of stock, but they can also continue later with a secondary public offering if they need to raise more capital.

A company that has stock that's performing well is usually considered a stable company and tends to have an easier time raising money through lenders, as well, aside from the sale of stock.

The stock market

The stock market is the place where stocks and bonds are "traded" (bought and sold). Simply put, a stock market links buyers and sellers, facilitating the exchange of securities between these two groups of investors.

A stock market may be termed as a physical place where face-to-face trading happens, such as the New York Stock Exchange in New York City, or more likely a virtual location, or a network where trades are made electronically.

There are two aspects of the stock market: the primary market and the secondary market.

The primary market is where new issues of stock are sold through the aforementioned initial public offerings or IPOs. Institutional investors – those who have extremely large dollar amounts to spend – use the primary markets to purchase shares at initial public offerings and are given preferential treatment due to the dollar amount they plan to purchase.

The secondary market is where the "little guy" makes his or her purchases. After the IPO, all subsequent trading happens on the secondary market, with offerings available to individual purchasers.

Chapter 2: Investing Versus Trading

Most individuals use the terms "investing" and "trading" interchangeably, inferring that the two are synonymous with one another. However, those well-versed in penny stocks know that they're two markedly different things that entail various risks, different time commitments, and most certainly some mixed results.

Being an Investor

Investing in penny stocks without doing lots of constant trading requires an individual with plenty of patience. Investors tend to "let it ride" rather than cashing out for small gains. The investor is the researcher and the wearer of rose-colored glasses. He's in it for the duration and, as such, stands to make more considerable gains than the trader.

Investing is wise in the penny stock market, especially for those new to the realm. Though it tends to be easier than being a trader, that doesn't mean there isn't work involved. The work tends to be more up-front at the beginning of the investment process. For example, an investor needs to jump into the often tedious task of investigating penny stock companies in which he would like to invest. This involves making calls, poring over figures, and putting it all together to make wise purchasing decisions. This takes time to do correctly but generally results in a better feeling about the stock purchased. Potentially, there may be less risk involved, as well.

Investors stand to recognize more gains than traders, because they tend to keep shares for a longer amount of time and, hence, they see prices rise over and over again rather than jumping to cash in at the first or second gain, fearing that it might be their only chance.

Most experts note that investing really is the best approach in the penny stock market.

Being a Trader

While the investor is the painter content to hone his masterpiece a few strokes at a time over several months, the trader is the child who spends his money as soon as he gets it without waiting to amass a considerable sum with which he could buy something much bigger - if only he had the patience. However, for him, those small rewards are much more exciting.

Traders are in it for the short-term gains and are discontent with waiting to see what happens. They are impatient players who rarely take the time to thoroughly research each penny stock company as investors do. Therefore, they depend mostly on the information available on trading charts to make their decisions about which shares to buy and which to pass up.

You might think that this takes less work. Well, it certainly does at the beginning of the process. Trading demands a much more active role in the health of one's stock portfolio. Because traders are only looking to make these short-term gains, they spend much more time buying and selling. They may even buy and sell several times in a day or dozens of times per week. For them, it's a nail-biting process they enjoy being part of that allows for perhaps a 10 or 20 percent gain each time (small tidbits that are less likely to result in significant profits, even over the long stretch). Nonetheless, it's a game that keeps the adrenaline pumping.

Again, investing is the better strategy for the novice, especially one who has entered the market with some trepidation; but trading - with all of its excitement - seems to be best suited for those who have a considerable amount of stock market know-how, even if that know-how hasn't been developed in the world of penny stocks.

Chapter 3: The Basics of Penny Stocks

Penny stocks are the gateway to a hidden sector of the stock market. Penny stocks differ from other types of stocks in that they're open to public investment, but they do not become available before they are a well-known brand. The reason that companies open themselves to investment before they are popular is to secure funding and continue developing a product. As a penny stock investor, you are investing in a company at its early levels of developing its product. It is for this very reason that penny stocks can be so profitable - you are a starting investor and have the opportunity to earn returns far greater than on any well known publicly traded stock.

Penny stocks get their name from their price. Although the Securities and Exchange Commission officially defines a penny stock as having a value of less than $5 per share, many penny stocks trade at or below $1 ('What are Penny Stocks and How Do Penny Stocks Work?', 2019). You will typically be buying penny stocks in large quantities of shares, but this does not mean that you will get majority ownership in nearly any penny stock company, nor would you want to do this. Nearly all of these small businesses have diluted the value of their shares; this is why they are worth so little individually. Also, their shares are not listed on most of the traditional stock exchanges. Most penny stocks are traded through the Over-The-Counter Bulletin Board and the Pink Sheets. If they were to become a corporation with influence all around the world, a long process would take place. To make money consistently and quickly, you won't be worried about companies that progress this far. The goal is to be interested only in the very beginning stages and then to get out of the market before the company becomes more popular.

The products that penny stock companies produce are vast and diverse. Businesses exist in everything from social media websites, to a chain of national party promoters, to a company that works to create more accurate global positioning systems. What is common amongst all of these companies is that large venture capital firms have passed on their ideas. Penny stock companies rely on a large swath of investors spread out across the country and the globe. Their market capitalization is a numbers game based on their total number of investors. Do not think all of these companies are destined to fail, although you should know that most of them will. For your purposes, you will be pulling out of a specific company long before they become a large success or before they fail and fade away.

The Securities and Exchange Commission has come to heavily regulate penny stocks in the last three decades. Many of these regulations regard starting investor count, the quality of market exchanges, and market capitalization prior to listing, which is a huge benefit to traders like you and me. There is one significant drawback to the added involvement of the SEC, however, and this is that they can stop trading on highly volatile stocks. There are specific cases of stock manipulation in the last twenty years that has put the SEC on high alert for penny stocks that are trading upwards in an irregular manner quickly. The SEC will halt trading on these stocks and will only reopen after they have looked at the underlying company being traded to see whether or not manipulation was used to raise the price. Yet again, the SEC has our best interests at heart, but this detail can be a real nuisance to traders.

When the SEC halts a stock, not only do traders lose the option to buy, but investors also cannot sell the stock that they've already purchased. The frequency of these events is limited, and this book will discuss specific strategies you can use should this ever happen. While it may seem like penny stocks have developed a bad name for themselves, you should understand that this view is extremely outdated and that present-day penny stock trading is generally well regulated, and investors are better protected. Actually, there is no better time to get involved in penny stocks than right now.

Traditional Markets

Traditional markets house large public companies that are known on an international scale. These are the companies that you've heard of, the companies that you shop at, and ones that might even include your employer. The traditional stock exchanges are very difficult to break through for many reasons, ranging from a lack of investor technology to limited capital, reducing potential profitability. Now, most trading is done online, and most trades are not executed by human beings. Mathematicians have created complicated algorithms that are programmed into a computer, executing trades based on complex theories about stock trends. These trades are conducted by the thousands per second, and they make it very difficult to compete. However, as a new trader, by far the biggest hurdle will not be technology, but rather a lack of capital.

Trades on standard stock exchanges are mostly made on very small margins per each share. To earn a good profit, you will need to purchase a lot of shares and invest thousands of dollars. Furthermore, to limit losses, you would ideally be purchasing options for sell prices in case the value drops, buy prices in case the stock continues to go up, and the entire time you will be dealing with numerous brokers - both online and over the phone. These are the reasons that most people eventually decide to invest in penny stocks. Most people have enough capital to create decent profits on good trades, but too many competitors are being replaced by machines. As a starting investor, stay away from these exchanges and look to penny stocks instead.

Why Penny Stocks Are So Profitable

Penny stocks are profitable because of their high volatility, their limited entry price, the size of the market, and the limits in human competitors. These are just some of the myriad of reasons these stocks are valuable for traders like you and me. Penny stocks are today what the traditional stock market was in the 1960s, 70s, and 80s - fast moving and taking on new investors every day. This increase in market capitalization spread out across various penny stocks is precisely why you'll be able to earn a decent profit through trading.

Today's large stock markets operate using a variety of complicated financial products, such as derivatives. These products were created to compensate for a slowing market or one that does not display as much volatility. As trading became more advanced and computers started making most trades, distance to the central exchanges become a prime concern, where investment firms are now purchasing property locked in New York City simply because they can make trades a hair of a second faster than their competitors.

This information does little to add why penny stocks are so profitable, but it does paint a picture of what has happened to traditional markets. As they have slowed down and grown more competitive, new tricks have been created by established investors that make profits much more difficult to come by for the average person. Penny stocks are an alternative that takes us back to the early days of the stock market where trades were done more slowly, and investors had more of an equal opportunity; this truly is why penny stocks are so profitable, especially compared to traditional markets.

Shortcomings of Penny Stocks

While the potential profit from penny stocks is good, you should also consider the disadvantages of investing in this kind of stock. Below we have outlined some of these downsides.

Most penny stock exchanges do not require companies to submit regular reports - Companies listed in the major stock exchanges are required to pass regular financial reports. The transparency of the companies' financial dealings allows investors to make informed decisions regarding when to buy and sell stocks.

Because penny stocks are not listed with major exchanges, these companies aren't required to submit reports. Financial news companies also do not give a lot of attention to these small companies. When investing in them, you should be the one doing the research regarding the nature of the business of the companies you invest in.

Aside from the financial reports, it may also be difficult to find information about the leadership and history of the companies you are investing in. You need to call these companies or go straight to their offices to gather this information. Learning about the leadership and history of a company is also important because they provide you with clues on the progress the company has made.

With bigger companies listed with the major exchanges, you can check the history of the company for bankruptcy and changes in leadership online. Their business transactions are well documented by the media. You can also check the track record of the company's current leaders. With a penny stock company, this information may not be available. A company that's trying to hide its past will successfully do so in this market.

The market may lack liquidity - The lack of market liquidity is a common problem in the penny stock market. Investing in major stock exchanges is easy because there are always buyers for the stocks you are selling. Even if local investors are feeling cautious about investing, there are always international investors who are interested in buying US shares.

International funds are not interested in buying

penny stocks due to their extremely speculative nature. The lack of information for companies listed in this market makes investing in them too risky for most institutional investors.

Due to insufficient players in the market, you may discover there are no buyers for the stocks you want to sell, especially when the market is down. The lack of buyers will push the prices down, which will lead to major losses on your part.

The Pump and Dump Scheme

Because of the low liquidity in the penny stock market, it's also easier for organized crime groups to execute a pump and dump scheme with certain penny stock companies.

This is an illegal practice in the stock market where a group of stockbrokers or marketing companies buy a big chunk of the stocks of a company when the prices are still low. The sudden buying up of large amounts of shares of the said company increases its market value. Using their sales teams, these groups increase the hype further for the company by offering its stocks for sale through the phone, fake news, newsletters, and other means of marketing.

They target people who can afford to buy the funds but who are not financially savvy enough to invest in the penny stock market. When these people check the stocks that the sales team is offering, they may see an upward trend in its prices. Because of this, many beginning investors may be fooled into buying the shares of the company.

The continued promotion of the shares of the company keeps fueling its price increase. This is the pump part of the process. When the price of the shares gets to a given point, the masterminds of the scheme begin to dump their shares of the company while the prices are still high. They also use their marketing teams to dispose of their shares. Due to owning a large chunk of the company, selling their shares affects the price of the shares.

When the masterminds of these schemes sell all of their shares, they stop marketing the stocks. The hype for the shares also decreases, and people start to sell the ones they own. However, the share prices will now be lower than their buying price. Usually, late buyers are the ones that suffer from most of the losses in these schemes.

While the SEC keeps an eye out for pump and dump schemes in the stock exchange, it is difficult for them to differentiate true investors from pump and dump masterminds. The task is even more challenging in the penny stock market. The lack of liquidity in the market makes it easier for criminal groups to fake price increases in the market.

Chapter 4: Personality Traits of a Successful Penny Stock Investor

Penny stocks are clearly not for everyone. Many investors prefer safer investments that are likely to grow steadily over long periods of time and have almost no chance of going belly-up. The penny stock investor is cut from a slightly different cloth. If you're wondering whether or not you're a penny stock investor in your heart of hearts, then consider the following factors (Leeds, 2019).

Do you enjoy actively managing and monitoring your portfolio?

The typical medium-to-large cap investor (someone who buys stocks in larger companies) doesn't really need to spend too much time researching their investments and monitoring their day-to-day performance. Perhaps once a quarter, they'll make some trades and evaluate how their stocks have performed, but it won't be a particularly heady endeavor. The successful penny stock investor, by contrast, actively monitors and manages their portfolio. They know that even if a penny stock looks good one week, a few factors can shuffle around quite quickly, and the stock will look like a disaster the next week. This investor will want to get out before it's too late. This type of active monitoring and frequent buying and selling requires time and also money, as you'll presumably be paying more commission for more frequent trading.

Will you be satisfied with a modest return?

It's important to set up reasonable expectations for your penny stock investment. Since there's so much hype behind penny stocks, many new investors expect big returns right out of the gate. The odds that you're going to stumble upon a big winner are incredibly low. If you're smart and diligent, then you have a decent chance of seeing some modest growth in the value of your portfolio over time. It is an incorrect assumption that you'll get rich quickly by investing in penny stocks.

Can you tell when someone's lying to you?

A good penny stock investor needs to have an adequate internal lie detector because a lot of lies get flung around in this space. Get ready to confront and size up a lot of over-hyped reviews about how a certain company is poised to change the world and the like. Stories are important, but you should never make an investment based on that alone. You're going to need to see important financial metrics, such as price-to-book, price-to-sales, and other important measurements that allow you to size up the company's true potential. This book discusses these and other metrics in the subsequent chapters. However, for now, just know that you can't be gullible if you want to succeed as a penny stock investor.

Do you cope well with risk?

If you're delving into penny stocks, then you need to accept that there's a certain amount of risk involved. You may wind up watching your investments go up in smoke left and right, but you may also watch them multiply aggressively. If you flinch at risks and prefer securities that are more, well, secure, then penny stocks may not be for you. As a good rule of thumb, you should only invest in penny stocks if you have enough disposable income to support your investments. If you're taking money out of crucial household budgets, such as rent, food, or your car payment, in order to buy more penny stocks, then you're acting irresponsibly.

Are you okay with letting it ride?

Unlike larger securities, penny stocks are not so easily liquidated. For common stocks, you can usually buy or sell on any day that the market is open. Penny stock investors don't enjoy the same level of liquidity. You may find yourself in the incredibly frustrating position of watching your stock rise aggressively but being unable to sell it before it dips back down again. This just comes with the territory.

Chapter 5: Pink Sheets

Pink sheets are termed as an OTC market that enables the electronic connectivity of broker and dealers; everything, including price quotes, is done virtually (Murphy, 2019). There is no trading floor required. However, because of the virtual environment pink sheet trading has to offer, it differs from the New York Stock Exchange (NYSE). The required criteria for pink sheet-listed companies aren't the same as the required criteria for companies listed on the NYSE (LIOUDIS, 2019). Because of these innate differences, you'll want to spend some time familiarizing yourself with the nature of pink sheets. That is what we'll to discuss in the following chapter - the securities, benefits, risks, and profitability ratios pink sheet trading has to offer to investors.

Who Can Be Pink Sheet-Listed?

Generally speaking, you'll find that most pink sheet-listed companies are small companies either starting out or struggling to obtain positive profit margins. They're typically thinly traded, tightly held companies. Especially for the struggling company, pink sheet trading is a bonus, as companies that are pink sheet-listed don't need to meet or maintain any particular requirements in order to obtain or remain pink sheet-listed. In order to be listed, all an interested company needs to do is submit a Form 211 with the OTC Compliance Unit with the current financial information included - that's it.

You should know that when you delve into the world of pink sheet trading, you'll find that some companies eagerly and willingly show you their financial books—their financial records, so to speak—while others don't. Unfortunately, pink sheet-listed companies are not obligated or required to show you their books upon request. You'll also inevitably encounter problems with finding annual reports on pink sheet-listed companies that interest you since these companies don't file the yearly or periodic reports as required. Unfortunately for the investor (you), this makes it nearly impossible to gain all the necessary financial information regarding the company of interest; unless they're willing to give it to you, of course.

The Difference between Pink Sheets and OTCBB

Whereas OTCBBs, a topic we learned about in the previous chapter, are owned and operated by NASDAQ, pink sheets are owned by private companies; and because OTCBB is organized by

NASDAQ, the second largest exchange platform in the world, it makes sense that strict rules, regulations, and standards follow. It's compulsory for issuers, for example, to register with the Securities and Exchange Commission. No registration is required for pink sheet-listed companies, nor do such rules or regulations exist.

The Benefits of Pink Sheets

Pink sheets can be extremely cheap per share, with some even costing less than a dollar. This makes pink sheet trading highly beneficial and incredibly advantageous to the potential investor looking to invest in small increments while wishing to reap potentially high financial rewards. Volatility levels are very high with pink sheets, so increases in even penny amounts may result in great financial returns for an investor.

If you're looking to reap dramatic benefits and are willing to take oftentimes bold financial risks in order to do so, you might want to look for companies that have recently suffered from negative financial events but that have the potential to make a comeback. Companies that were once listed on the NYSE, for example, might be good starting points. You can purchase shares from those companies and hope that they make a comeback.

One of the best things about pink sheet-listed companies is that you can invest your money in a small or unpopular company, but still achieve a positive return rate. If a company is small and less known, you have a higher chance of success, because the competition is low. Investing in these small companies can turn out to be quite profitable if the growing process continues over time. In the future, and with gradual growth, that same company might be listed on a key exchange.

Risks Associated with Pink Sheets

As an investor, you should be well aware that there can be many disadvantages to pink sheet trading, as well - especially when investment opportunities and endeavors are approached in inappropriate or unknowledgeable ways. One of the biggest disadvantages of pink sheet trading is the limited amount of information that listed companies are required to share with investors and dealer-brokers. A company's decision to not report their financial status or publish annual reports makes it far more difficult for investors to access the information they require to consider the company, make vital financial decisions, and take risk-free actions. In other words, without these annual reports, you will not have all the crucial information about what you are purchasing and how the company is doing.

These pink sheet-listed companies are also thinly traded. You can purchase 500 shares from a company that promises to become the next Microsoft, but what happens if you gain a good profit and then decide to sell? When you sell, the price of the stock goes down. When a large number of investors continually do this, stocks and companies gain the title of being thinly traded. Regardless of what the market is when you do decide to sell, if you don't find a potential buyer for your stocks, you won't be able to get out of the position you put yourself in.

This situation becomes even more complicated when it comes to pink sheet-listed companies. It's a hard task to initiate a stock position when the bid-ask spreads are high. If you want to invest in those companies, you should be aware of the fact that they usually may not be covered by analysts. For example, if you watch or read the daily financial news, you'll already know that they almost never cover companies that aren't listed on a major exchange. This means that you will need to do some extra research in order to find the important information you need to make knowledgeable decisions and take successful actions.

The Workings of the Pink Sheet Tier System

The tier system was mentioned synonymously with

the pink sheet trading system earlier, but let's stop for a second and take a closer look before moving on. In recent years, the pink sheet system has adopted something called "market tiers," an organizational method that lists and separates the companies that have higher risk levels from those with lower degrees of financial risk.

With these tiers, you can gain a sense of increased clarity regarding the type of company you are investing in (Beers, 2018). As its name suggests, there are certain levels, or tiers, that a company can fall under (Basenese, 2017). There are five in total, which are detailed below.

Tier #1: Trusted Tiers - Just like their name suggests, these tiers are confirmed by the pink sheet OTC market to be trustworthy and highly appealing to investors. The companies that fall under this tier have both international companies and ones in the US. With this in mind, the trusted tier can then be divided into two sub-categories, as follows:

- **International Premier QX**: These consist of overseas companies that are listed on an international exchange, though they still cover the required financials of the listed worldwide standards noted and regulated by the NYSE. These companies conduct an independent audit and are able to present an immediate CEO certification to anyone who refuses to comply with corporate governance.

- **Premiere QX:** This includes companies that are based only in the US and continually meet the standards of NASDAQ's capital market. It is not necessary for those companies to report directly to SEC, although they have to adhere to the requirements that NASDAQ lists.

Tier #2: Transparent Tiers - Transparent tiers are below the trusted tier. It consists of:

- **OTCBB pink quotes**: This represents companies that are listed on both the OTCBB and pink sheet systems. OTCBB makes it necessary for these companies to give frequent reports to the SEC.

- **OTCBB:** As you've learned throughout this book already, these companies are simply found on the OTCBB market only.

- **Information right now**: Such companies have daily and current information, meaning that they provide the given information with the OTC Disclosure or the Securities and Exchange Commission. The information that's provided is less than six months old. If a company wants to keep itself up on this exact tier and not move down, it needs to file an annual report within the period of 75 days after the ending of the final quarter. The information will be verified as posted by the pink sheets OTC market.

Tier #3: Distressed Tiers - These are next on the

tier and are tough to manage. The companies listed within this tier include:

- **Companies with limited information:**

  - The information that's listed may be available for everyone to view, but it is generally older than six months and often doesn't meet the pink sheets OTC market requirements.

  - A company might file a report to SEC, but they still haven't kept that report updated frequently.

  - Broken and bankrupted companies oftentimes pop up on this list. These companies must promptly file information with both the News Service and OTC Disclosure.

Tier #4: Defunct Tiers - Only two kinds of companies are included in the defunct tiers:

- **Companies without information**: This category can be easily recognized by its stop signal sign. Companies that fall under this tier are either defunct or haven't filed any kind of update on current information to the OTC Disclosure, the Securities and Exchange Commission, or the News Service in the last six months. If you are considering any investment in these types of companies, proceed with caution.

- **Gray markets:** This second market, much like the previous tier category, has its own symbol, too, and that is the exclamation point. The companies listed in the gray market are missing a market maker and are not listed on either OTCBB or pink sheets. As a bonus, there is no transparency within the markets.

Tier #5: Toxic Tiers - Just like the name indicates, toxic tiers are tiers that have an extremely high level of risk. Its symbol, the skull and crossbones, suggests the risk investors take when pursuing companies listed within this tier. Only one category falls under this tier:

- **Caveat emptor:** The translation of this tier's title to English is quite clear: "buyer beware." On pink sheets, these tiers are described as stocks that can be a scam, have an unclear promotion, undergo regular suspensions, and many other things that reveal their risk level. Many of the companies listed within this bottom-most tier are all too often scams.

Now that you know a little more about the 5 types of tiers within the investing and penny stocks world, you need to learn about the brokers. That is, if you decide to invest in pink sheet stocks, you should consider hiring a broker. If you have already made a broker account, your broker is supposed to grant you an allowance to trade pink sheet stocks. However, be aware that this might not be possible, as some brokerage companies can only grant their most loyal customers to trade in the pink sheet market. If you do find an opportunity to delve into the pink sheet trading market with the help of your broker, you will be asked to sign another form that states that you understand and agree that pink sheet stocks can be risky investment endeavors.

There are many companies out there who simply don't want to give out any information concerning their business and financial matters. Be careful about investing in companies like this. Pink sheet companies are highly appealing due to their low price, and many investors find them interesting investment opportunities because they want to step up into a current and potentially rising company. The possibility that you may lose portions or all of your investment if you don't make the right buying choice means that you need to think carefully before proceeding with any decision.

You'll always want to avoid speculative stocks. Pink sheet trading has made major progress in the last few decades, and there have been more standards set, and there is more information circulating about pink sheet-listed companies, thanks to the help of the OTC market. If a pink sheet-listed company is introduced to one of the tier systems we discussed earlier, the more likely an investor will find it to be attractive. Be sure to pay attention to the tier system you select and ask for professional help before making any financial decisions. Be wary of some of the "expert" advertisements, as many are unreliable or scams. Sit down and do the research yourself. You can also take a look at the OTC Markets Group website; they have a detailed list of many OTC stocks. For now, though, you'll want to focus mostly on the two main stock categories: OTCQX and OTCQB. The other categories will not provide much information, and there may not be many strategies for them.

Chapter 6: Getting Started

Now, you have come to the part of this book where you will learn all there is to know about starting your penny stock trading venture. You might think that penny stock trading is complicated, with all the rules, things to look out for, complicated stock exchange terms, and everything else involved, but it is actually quite simple (Murphy, 2018). Read on to find out the four basic steps in starting your undertaking in penny stocks.

Research

Like when you start doing anything that you are unfamiliar with, you first need to do some research. In this book, the word "research" refers to two kinds of research. Before going to battle, you must first get your weapon ready, and in the world of penny stocks, there's no better weapon than knowledge.

The first kind of research is general research. This involves gathering general information about penny stocks, such as what it entails, how to go about investing in them, and most especially, the risks involved. Through this book, you ought to already have the proper knowledge for your general penny stock research.

The second type of research is the specific stock research. This kind of research should be done when you're actually looking for prospective penny stocks to invest in. Researching about the stock you are going to invest in should essentially be done when dealing with all kinds of stocks, but this is especially important for penny stocks. That's because, as you might recall from the previous sections, information about penny stocks is quite lacking and more difficult to find when compared to other kinds of stocks.

While researching about penny stocks, there are two things you need to look for. For one, you should look for any accessible public data about the stock. The second thing you need to look for is information regarding the stock's historical performance. While looking for this, you should observe and take note of the kinds of events that occurred and the reactions of the share price. An example of these events was instances when the price of the share remained as it was when there should have been an increase. An event such as this may suggest that investors have looked over the stock's information and decided to steer clear from investing in the stock.

Choose a Broker to set up an Online Brokerage Account

As soon as you have done enough research, the next

thing to do in order to start your penny stock investments is to set up your own brokerage account just as you would at a bank. A brokerage account is a platform from where you will be able to buy stocks and other investments. It's also here that your money will be held, along with your investments. When you buy shares, your money will be taken out of your account and exchanged for company shares. Then, when you successfully sell your shares, they will be converted into money.

There are different kinds of brokerage accounts out there. One kind is brokerage accounts that you can manage yourself, though this is not recommended for beginners. For novice penny stock investors, it's best to select a broker for yourself. These paid professionals will be the people who directly buy or sell your stocks as they are told. Of course, you also have to provide them with their payment, called "commissions" or "commission fees." These payments can range from $5 to prices in the hundreds.

Two types of brokers exist that you can choose from full-service stock brokers (known as traditional brokers) and discount stock brokers.

Full-service brokers offer a much more extensive array of services, including the offering of advice and suggestions on what shares to buy and which investment can be more profitable for you. Due to these services, traditional brokers tend to have a higher commission fee compared to discount brokers. Enlisting these kinds of brokers is only good for investors who plan to do only a few trades and can afford to spend a lot of money. If money is a concern for you, hiring a full-service stockbroker is not advisable. Commission fees for brokers like these can cost you around $100 for purchasing stocks and an additional $100 for selling, and that doesn't even include other service fees.

A good choice for beginning investors would be to employ discount stock brokers. Although they offer a very limited number of services, you'll have more freedom when it comes to making decisions. If you prefer to be more independent in your decision-making process, you should opt to hire discount stock brokers, as their services only include giving limited investment advice. Consequently, their commission fees are cheaper, and you as an investor can save more money.

A much better option for you would be online discount brokers, partnered with an online brokerage account. Using the power of the internet in these times will be to your advantage, as you will be the one mainly managing your account, and using the internet is the most effective way to do so. Online brokerage systems can help you keep an eye on your account and execute orders to your broker. Here, you can see market indexes, monitor buy orders that are open, stay updated on quoted stock prices, and obtain access to analyses and research done by your broker anytime you want help making your decisions. With this arrangement, you can save a lot of money on commission fees while also making your transactions simpler.

When you have finally chosen a broker, setting up your brokerage account will become much easier. You only have to contact your broker, and they will provide you with the forms or files that need to be filled out. Most of the time, they'll be the one who creates the account. Of course, you cannot start an account without an initial cash deposit or a minimum investment. This can range from a few hundred dollars to around $1,000. After this, your account will be up and running in approximately three to four days, and you can then start investing.

Buy

After setting up the brokerage account, the next step is to start buying stocks. This is the most crucial part in the course of all your penny stock transactions. The moment you make the mistake of buying and investing in the wrong stocks, you are already bound to lose money.

Buying stocks is quite simple. When you want to purchase shares of stocks, you should first contact your broker and execute a buy order. However, before doing this, you must first ensure that your brokerage account is stocked up with an adequate amount of money - enough to be able to pay for the share costs and commissions that you will eventually incur.

When contacting your broker, you should have already done your research. You should also have the following set of information: the ticker symbol of the organization that executed the stock, the market that the stock is being traded in, the number of shares or the volume that you want to get, the price of the shares that you're prepared to pay, and the order's duration or how long you want it to last (it can be for only that specific day or until the date that you selected).

The ticker symbol is the trading symbol by which organizations are identified within the stock exchanges and bulletin boards. For example, you can tell your broker that you want to purchase 1,000 shares of a specific company with a ticker symbol HYPO at $1 or less. You can go on to say that the stock must be traded on the OTC Bulletin Boards, and you want this order to remain active until Thursday. By this time, what you need to do is wait; it's up to your broker to deal with the transaction.

So, if ever the price of HYPO shares becomes equal to or less than $1, your broker will purchase the shares. If you check on your online brokerage account, you'll discover that you already have 1,000 shares. Consequently, the money in your account, which will serve as payment for the shares and for the broker's commission fee, will also be transferred to the respective recipients - in this case, $1,000 to HYPO and approximately $5 to your broker.

You may now be wondering how you'll know if a certain penny stock is a good investment or not. Four of the primary things that you need to look out for in a penny stock are as follows:

1. The price range must be $0.50 to $2; stocks with prices higher than $2 in the Over-The-Counter Bulletin Board are a bit harder to find.

2. The daily average volume should not be less than 100,000 numbers of shares. (This will be discussed further in the next chapter.)

3. The stocks should be moving higher in the market.

4. Avoid stocks from companies with negative growth rates in earnings; you can obtain this information via data released to the public through the SEC or in listings.

Sell

Similarly to buying penny stocks, selling penny stocks is also very simple, though there is still a lot of information to take into account. As discussed in the third chapter, where we touched on the benefits and risks of penny stock trading, finding a buyer for penny stocks is quite difficult. However, having a broker to do the actual trading for you will make it much easier.

As in buying, all you need to do in order to sell your penny stocks is do a bit of research, contact your broker, and execute a sell order. Also, the information that you gave your broker for your buy order is the same as what you will have to give to them for your sell order. These include the ticker symbol, market, volume of shares you wish to sell, price of the shares, and the order's duration.

As an example, you can notify your broker that you want to sell 1,000 of your shares from your account in a specific company with the ticker symbol HYPO. You can then tell them that the stocks are in the OTCBB and that you wish to sell your stocks at $2 or more, with the order being active until the following Wednesday.

So, if the stock price of HYPO does become $2 or more, it will be sold. The money that's exchanged with the stock will be transferred to your account, and it can then be used for another transaction; however, this money will already be deducted with the broker's commission fee. Consequently, you now have $1,995 in your account.

If you want to know whether or not you made profits from your transactions, you can visit stocks and investment websites to help you gauge your profits, or you can do the computation yourself. To do this, just simply compare or subtract the money you shelled out for your buy order and the money you made from your sell order. For example, if the buy order cost you $1,005 ($1,000 for the stocks and $5 for the commission fee), and you got $1,995 for the sell order ($2,000 for the stocks, subtracted with $5 for the commission fee), after subtracting, you then have a profit of $990.

How to Open up an Account

The first step you'll need to follow when starting your investment in penny stocks is choosing which trading account you would like and then opening up the account. As an investor, it's in your best interest to take into consideration how easy the account is to work with. You should think about how easy it is to transfer to and from the account, the customer service that is offered with the account, and any fees that are associated with opening and running the account. There are times when a broker will choose a fixed rate for a smaller amount of shares, but one that can increase when trading on more shares. Depending on the type of trading that you do, this could make a big difference in the profit you make.

The nice thing about working on a commission per share idea is that it works well for investors who want to get into penny stocks but don't have a lot of extra money for this. As the investor, you will need to shop around in order to find the best broker and the best trading account to help expand your options and maximize your profits, so take the time to look at and talk to a few different companies to determine which one is the best for you to open.

Starting with Paper Trading

To start paper trading, you can go to online broker companies that provide practice software for prospective investors. You should choose companies that do not require initial deposits to download their software. By starting with these companies, you'll also start learning how to use their trading software.

If for some reason this method is not accessible, you could start paper trading manually. All you need is a notebook, a pen, and a stable internet connection. You can start paper trading by following these steps:

1.   Set a trading budget

You should start by setting a budget that is close to your real-world budget. By setting one like this, you will be able to learn the advantages and limitations set by your budget. Ideally, you should choose an even number like $1,000 or $5,000. These numbers are easier to remember, and they will make it easier to calculate your profits or losses.

2.   Set your trading rules

It's also possible to make the trading experience more realistic by setting real-world rules for your practice trading. For instance, you could start by setting the fees of your chosen broker. To learn about these fees, you can shop around for legitimate penny stock brokers. Try asking investors that you know of for recommendations. If you don't know people who invest in penny stocks, you can also try reading some blogs written by penny stock traders.

Aside from the fees, you should also consider jotting down the sources of information that you will use when buying and selling penny stocks. The best information source varies depending on the industry that you're participating in. You should also consider looking into the analytic tools that you'll use in making your decision when picking stocks and timing your selling process. These will be discussed in future chapters.

It's best to focus on one specific sector. By focusing on the healthcare sector, for example, you will be able to limit the amount of time you spend on research and information gathering. You will be able to specialize in your research because you will then have more time to delve into the companies. If you don't focus on one sector or industry, you'll spend all of your time on this task alone. The sheer number of companies out there will end up overwhelming you.

3. Use the best methods for practice trading

When investing in penny stocks, you need to follow certain rules that will increase your chances of making a profit. We have outlined some of these rules below:

- Set a target amount - You should have a goal when investing. A good investor sets his eyes on his goal and never gives up until he achieves it. Your goal will also result in an easier decision-making process. Let's say you want to increase your $100,000 practice money to $150,000. You will need a 50 percent increase in your investment. If you increase your portfolio value by 5 percent every month, you'll reach your goal within your eighth month. If you would like to attain your goal faster, you will need to take more risks by buying stocks with higher interest rate potential.

  You will learn about the potential of these penny stocks based on their performance when you practice buying and selling them. By practicing your stock picking skills, you will be able to figure out which stocks perform well before you start risking real money. You will also have an idea of the spectrum of potential in investing in your chosen sector. This will prevent you from setting unrealistic goals when you're already using real money.

- Practice buying stocks only in your chosen sectors - When practicing investing in penny stocks, focus your resources only in your chosen sectors. If you plan to invest in the finance and healthcare sectors, for instance, only focus your practice time in them. This will develop your discipline in investing. When investing with real money, you'll be tempted to buy stocks that are hyped.

Don't feel bad if you missed out on these stocks because they are merely distractions. Instead, focus on the stocks of companies that you're familiar with. This way, you will always be making informed decisions rather than gambling away your money.

- Don't put your money in one company - When practicing, you should make a point to diversify your investments. Beginning investors are always tempted to throw their money into "sure" profits. However, you should learn from this point that there are no sure profits, especially in penny stocks. Because of the lack of information, penny stock companies post higher risks. The risk that comes with this type of investment makes diversifying even more important.

Start developing the discipline to diversify your resources, even when practicing, so that you won't be tempted by big profits when using real money.

- Follow more than one penny stock company at once - In the beginning, you should start following just a handful of companies. For instance, you should begin by following five companies from your chosen penny stock list.

These companies should belong to your chosen sectors. As you spend more time following the market, you can expand the number of companies that you're following in these sectors. Eventually, you will know how each company stock performs in specific economic conditions.

Observe how the stock of these companies performs when the market is down. Take note of the best-performing stocks when the market is bullish and also when the market is bearish.

4. Start buying and selling penny stocks

Now that you have set the trading criteria, you can now start going through the list of your chosen exchange and start researching about the companies that you find interesting. Your goal is to find a company that may be undervalued in the market. You can learn more about the company through research. With the internet, information flows faster. However, many individuals are looking for information about penny stock companies. You want to learn about key information before the rest of the market catches on.

When practicing, you should use your short-term, mid-term, and long-term strategies. Set a budget, and pick stocks that you will buy and sell in the short-term. You will buy and sell these stocks within the next month. You should also select stocks for your mid-term strategy. You will hold these penny stocks for at least one month and up to six months.

You should consider penny stocks for long term investments, as well. These investments are held for at least six months. You will need to hold especially stable companies for long term investments. These companies should have a great product and strong corporate leaders, and they should also show an intention for expansion. This can be in the arrangement of new products to reach new markets. They could also be expanding to more places. In some cases, they may realign their marketing strategy to target new market segments.

If you see that a company is successful in these types of business activities, you may want to consider investing in them for longer periods. In some cases, companies may even transition out of their penny stock status and register in a bigger exchange. This will increase the company's exposure and the value of its stock.

5. Record your thoughts and experiences

When practicing, your goal is to create a list of guidelines to follow when you are already investing with real money. To do this, you need to record the strategies that you use and the changes that you create along the way. Start by using an investment journal. Choose a dotted journal where you record your thoughts before buying or selling stocks. After each week, record the results of the strategies you used. You should also include additional notes regarding your thoughts on specific strategies, companies, and economic events.

Let's say you practiced buying 100 shares of Company A and 100 shares of Company B. The market was on a downtrend all week long. Company A behaved accordingly, and your 100 shares decreased in value by 1.5 percent. However, Company B performed opposite to the performance of the market, and it increased in value by 0.5 percent.

You should take note of these factors in your journal. You could note the respective performances of these companies in your journal in that week and compare their performance to the overall performance of the sector and the market.

By doing so, you will get an idea of how stocks from certain companies behave during bullish and bearish markets. If the entire sector increased in value by 50 percent and your investment strategies only appreciated by 20 percent, you might be missing out on some key stocks. If you're participating in only one sector, use the sector performance as a gauge of your success. If you play in multiple sectors, on the other hand, use the performance of the market as your gauge.

Take note of the things that you should have done to improve your performance. Consider all risk and reward exchanges when you are noting your experiences. Your insights when practice trading may make you a lot of money when you're already investing real money.

6.   **Assess the best and worst trades weekly**

When trading, you'll want to have a reason for each of your actions. You'll also want to know why the market behaved the way it did. You will learn these insights through experiences in the market.

You can start understanding these insights even while only still practicing. Every week, you should assess your trading performance and try to explain each of your actions, writing them down in your journal. Write down your thought process for why you bought or sold a certain stock of a company.

Aside from this, you should also assess the performance of the companies you bought and sold. Try to explain why a certain company increased in value. If a company performed less than expected, try to explain why it did that.

In this part of the process, you should also assess the value of your information sources. You should keep track of the information that you use when taking trading actions. If the information from a source keeps turning out to be false, drop the source. When using real money, only listen to sources of information that consistently churn out reliable data.

7. Adjust your strategy based on your personal preferences

When you transition to real money, the fear of losing tends to set in and affect your performance. Take note of the mental factor when investing. More importantly, adjust your strategy based on the changes in your mindset. If you are afraid of losing money, you may perform better if you avoid high-risk stocks or if you transition into a sector with fewer price fluctuations.

If you're invested in tech stocks, for instance, you may be shocked by the sharp price fluctuations of the companies in the sector. These fluctuations will be even greater if you enter the market in an active season. If the fluctuations in the prices of stocks in this sector make you anxious, try practicing in less active sectors, such as the food industry.

Transitioning to Investing with Real Money

After practicing for months or even years, the next step is to process your application to start investing with real money. You need to consider a couple of things:

- Budget - Your budget should cover the initial investment required by your broker. It's possible to invest more, but as this is your first time, it's recommended that you start small. Some brokers have penalties for accounts that have low balances, so make sure that you have this amount covered to avoid unnecessary fees.

- Look for a broker that fits your needs - When selecting a broker, you should pick one according to the type of service that you need. In most cases, you will deal with regular brokers. They don't specify that they cater to only penny stock investors. However, take note of the ones who have special services for penny stock traders.

You will usually find special treatment to penny stock traders based on the fees and requirements that the broker imposes. Here are some of the fees and special requirements:

1. Minimum balance

If you are just starting out and testing your strategies, you may want to begin with discount brokers. These include brokers with no minimum balance requirements. You can start investing in penny stocks for as low as $100.

2. Commission rate per trade

As you become more active, you may want to choose a broker with a low per-trade commission rate. You should shop around for the perfect balance between the minimum balance requirement and the per-trade commission rate.

3. Fees for low-priced shares

Since we're focusing on penny stocks, you should also avoid brokers that impose fees for low-priced shares. Some brokers have these types of fees to make more money from penny stocks and to discourage penny stock trading.

Choosing a Broker

So you've made it this far. You've read through the pros and cons of penny stock trading and somehow managed to avoid being scared away by the fact that it's so risky. Perhaps you're even enthralled by the possibilities that come along with penny stock trading or the inherent challenge. Well, that's perfect! Before we delve into how to pick the perfect stock in order to multiply your money and hopefully make you millions, there's one essential pit stop that we need to make: choosing the broker that we're going to decide on (Murphy, 2019).

The broker that you decide to use will actually have a lot of sway on the whole process of your trading. Your choice of broker can make a definite difference in how much money you make. You're going to want different brokers depending upon the exact situation that you're working with. For example, if you only have $500 to invest, you obviously don't want a broker with a $1,000 account minimum.

There are a few specific things that you want to be mindful of when you're choosing between various different online penny stock brokers.

The first thing is surcharges. Different brokers will

often add surcharges to stocks if they cost less than a certain amount of money. The charges that aren't necessarily huge - usually something like a one-cent surcharge for every share bought - can still add up, especially if you're trading in higher volumes.

Another thing to be aware of is that a lot of brokers put restrictions in place. These may pop up as either restrictions to the volume that you trade or the manner in which you trade. When brokers restrict the volume of your trades, they'll often charge quite a bit extra for particularly large stock purchases. When they restrict the manner in which you trade, there are a myriad of ways in which they can do this. For example, some may require you to call them in order to place an order of a certain size, while others may demand that you only trade so many times per day. Neither is convenient, but sadly, it's the reality of working with online brokers. However, many online brokers won't have such stringent regulations in place, and you can rest assured that the regulations that are there are there for a certain reason.

So what broker will you go with? It depends on exactly what you need.

Overall

Many consider the two best penny stock brokers overall to be Charles Schwab and E-Trade. As an added perk to their other benefits, they both have a very strong customer support team and offer a ton of resources to educate you on how to choose stocks and play the market on your terms.

Charles Schwab is fantastic for a number of reasons. First off, they have a relatively low trade commission of only $4.95 for every trade you issue. The platform that they've established for trading penny stocks is top-notch and will definitely not leave you wanting. The only downside of Charles Schwab is that they have an account minimum of $1,000, which may be a bit out of your grasp, depending on whether you're wanting to get into this trade as a hobby or not. However, bear in mind that compared to some others (which we'll look at momentarily), this still isn't a bad account minimum. If you have the initial speculative investment capital to spend, then Charles Schwab is certainly a great option. As an added bonus, as of the time of writing, Charles Schwab will give you $500 cash with which to do as you wish if you deposit a certain amount of money into your account.

The other overall best option is often considered to be E-Trade. Their trade commission is a little bit higher than Charles Schwab's, clocking in at $6.95 per trade, but it falls down to be equal to Charles Schwab's at $4.95 if you issue more than thirty trades every financial quarter. If you intend on trading more heavily and more often, this may be the ideal route for you. The fact that they benefit people who intend to trade frequently even extends into their current promotion: they will give you sixty days of trades without any commission at all if you deposit a certain amount of money. What does this mean for you? Well, it means that if you're a frequent trader, then you could save hundreds of dollars on trade commissions. There are a lot of reasons that you can benefit from using E-Trade, but the low trade commissions combined with an easy-to-use and powerful platform, alongside an amazing breadth of penny stocks to choose from and a Library of Alexandria's worth of important information for enterprising young traders, all make it a great option.

Low Commissions

If you're specifically looking for brokers who will have a very light footprint on the amount you spend on commissions, then there are two other options you might want to consider. The ones with the lowest commission footprints are typically said to be Merrill Edge and Interactive Brokers.

Merrill Edge has a relatively high base commission at $6.95 per trade, but they don't have any sort of surcharges on top of that. That is to say that, on top of the cost that you're paying for your shares, you pay $6.95, and that's it. So where does Merrill Edge fall short? There aren't many, but one thing that you may find a tad out of reach is their $25,000 account minimum. Merrill Edge also certainly does not take any pains to cater to people who want to play the penny stock market. They allow people with lesser account values to trade on the normal exchanges and also have a mandate that money placed in penny stocks shouldn't be more than 20 percent of their account minimum. Despite all of this, if low commissions are your game, then Merrill Edge just may be the option that you want to look into.

Interactive Brokers is the other choice that has a very light commission footprint. They have no extra charges for penny stocks beyond a $1 minimum payment on every order that you place and a $0.50 cent per share commission. This is not much at all. You could trade 800 shares before it even really touches the base commission of other services, and that's not even including other services' surcharges and costs of a similar nature. They also have a much lower account minimum than Merrill Edge, coming in at only $10,000. However, they do quite a bit to vet the people that trade on their platform, wanting to keep it mainly used by professionals who have the money to spare. They have a monthly commission minimum of right around $10. They also require that you have a certain net worth and amount of income depending upon your age.

Platforms

If you're looking for the absolute best platform - maybe you're a hopeful professional or someone who just really wants to spend a lot of time analyzing the decisions that they make - then there are two services that you'd really be hard pressed to do much better than Ameritrade and TradeStation.

Ameritrade may just be one of the best platforms out there for a lot of reasons. They certainly don't cater to penny stock traders, with a pretty high trade commission of $6.95, but aside from that, they're actually a great choice for multiple reasons, the first of which being that they have no account minimum. Granted, you may pay for this later in surcharges and commission, but if you don't have much to get started and just want to be a weekend trader with some of the extra money you've got lying around, then you and Ameritrade just might become best friends. On top of that, they'll give you a $600 bonus when you deposit a certain amount of money.

We're not here to talk about any of that, though, are we? Ameritrade isn't being listed for its low account minimum nor its hefty promotional bonus. Rather, it's being mentioned for its absolutely incredible trading platform. Ameritrade's thinkorswim is easily one of the best trading platforms out there, regardless of what is being traded. It's equally great for options trading, safer securities trading, and penny stock trading, for the sole reason that thinkorswim is loaded with professional-grade tools that will help you do everything that you need to do and learn everything that you need to know. You'd be wise to try to work with Ameritrade in order to utilize it if a high-tech and limitless platform are among the things that you'd like to see in whatever broker that you choose. If you need something simpler for starting out, they also have an easily usable web interface called Trade Architect, which is far friendlier to newer investors.

TradeStation is the other broker worth mentioning for their platform. They have a trading platform that's immensely and endlessly complex. However, for its complexity, it is one of the most extensive and endlessly useful trading platforms on the market. Even more, it offers a plethora of tools and data that will help you figure out if you're making the right buy every single time.

Ending Notes

We have covered the most worthwhile penny stock brokers to look into. They all have their own sets of features that make them the best in their own right, and all of them have their own sets of pros and cons. I can't pin down the right one for you, simply because I'm not you. You could be a college student with an extra $1,000 from scholarships that you'd like to invest, or you could be a middle-aged man trying to make investments with some early pension money. It all depends on you and what you want out of investing.

How to Select Penny Stocks

In order for you as an investor to have a sense of clarity when it comes to what lies in store for your investment into penny stocks, it's helpful to know a stock's history. As the tried and true cliché goes, history repeats itself. Moving ahead without taking the time to look back will essentially doom you to make the same mistakes that other investors may have already made many times over. Generally speaking, some investors say that trading in penny stocks can simply be different scenarios that repeatedly play out time and again, generation after generation. Some investors are under the impression that the old economy rules will not work with new economy stocks, but no matter what your personal take on this issue may be, there is an irrefutable fact that researching the past proves for a more profitable future. How do you pick a winning penny stock? As stated previously in this book, it all begins with your research.

Share Price

Get to know that prices aren't always what they seem. The general line of logic is that penny stocks are far more cost-effective. However, this isn't necessarily true and fails to take other factors into account.

This is one of the biggest things that people misunderstand about penny stocks. Just because they're cheaper doesn't mean that they're automatically worth more, or that you're getting more for less. Allow me to explain.

People who reduce the entire situation to this simple notion of "share price" don't realize the actual value of their shares. This is where the concept of "shares outstanding" comes into play.

For example, let's consider two companies, one of which has a share price of $0.05 and a market capitalization of $50,000,000. The other has a share price of $50 and a market cap of $50,000,000. They have identical market capitalizations, so they are actually not faring too badly compared to one another in terms of investiture. Because the first company has a share price of $0.05 and a market cap of $50,000,000, we can surmise that they have 1,000,000,000 outstanding shares, with outstanding shares being defined as the number of shares that have currently been issued. This is different from "authorized shares," which is the number of shares that the company is allowed to issue by the marketplace regulations. Meanwhile, Company B only has 1,000,000 shares issued. Thus, even though the two companies have a similar market cap and are faring similarly in that respect, the shares of Company A have a lower price than the shares of Company B, by virtue of the fact that there are more of them. Thus, the price of a company's shares isn't necessarily indicative of how well it's faring, especially not compared to another with a higher share price.

Side note: market capitalization has two meanings in the world of finance. The first is the sum total of the value of a corporation's stock, alongside its long-term debt and the earnings that it has retained. However, it can also refer to the number of outstanding shares multiplied by the share price to indicate how many have invested in the company and at what price. Here, of course, we're using the second definition, as we normally will throughout these discussions.

Dilution

This is the other thing that a new trader needs to be wary of when working with penny stocks; perhaps even more experienced traders won't have that much of an idea about how this concept works. Dilution refers to when the number of shares outstanding increases drastically and uncontrollably. There are a lot of reasons that this might happen. Among the most common are when companies decide to issue shares to others. This happens most often when they offer their employees stock options or when they start issuing shares as a means to raise the amount of capital that they have.

The second is actually extremely common among small companies as a means to raise the amount of money that they have, which is needed to operate and glide by until they have a meaningful occurrence (product launch, company milestone, new facility, and so forth). However, when this happens, it can dilute the percentage of the company that's owned by the investors who contributed before the company began to issue shares. This would cause the share price to decline massively in order to maintain a steady market cap.

When you're working with penny stocks, it's incredibly important to be sure that the company you're wanting to use has a strong grip on the structure of its shares and the way that shares are supposed to be handled in different situations. If a company dilutes its shares constantly, the values of the shares will drop for the people who already own some. In other words, you won't be making money, and that's not a good thing. Be super careful about this. A company that dilutes often could make or break your penny stock portfolio.

How to Seek out the Winners

This is what you're reading this book for, I'm sure - to learn how to seek out penny stocks that will make you a lot of money in a short amount of time. Well, I can tell you that there's certainly no formula for doing so in any way, but there are a lot of things that you can do to increase the chances of picking a stock (or a set of stocks) that will give you a noticeable return.

First off, you need to look at how a company works. Look at the bare essentials of the company and its actions in order to determine whether it's a bright move or just a bold move for you to invest in them.

For example, if they dilute their share prices often by issuing shares, do you really want to invest? Look at their structure, too. Is the company either drawing a profit, or will it eventually be able to gain a profit just by looking solely at the structure of the business and their current plans? Is it a realistic investiture? Could you see yourself using their product, if it came down to it? Is the company able to make a meaningful statement within its sector? Meaning, will the company be able to compete at a decent level with its competitors and hopefully, come out on top? Research its competitors, too, and see if it genuinely stands an honest chance against them.

If you do this for every single stock that interests you, you almost certainly will be able to find a very promising company with a bright future ahead of it right then and there. It's actually incredible just how much context can do for you as an enterprising investor, so seek it out as much as you possibly can. Knowing the context of a company will help prevent you from making terrible and wasteful investments.

Yet another thing that you can do is consider whether or not the company is in a sector where it's common or reasonable for a stock to be trading for less than a dollar. For example, the mining industry tends to have a lot of companies that trade for extremely low amounts - sometimes even just pennies. Because certain sectors rely quite a bit on the issuing of new shares in order to raise capital alongside hurting from increased competition within the sector, a potential investor must stay very alert as to the specific conditions in which the business they'd like to invest is residing. If the business suffers from poor conditions in a poor sector, then they likely are not a wise investment. If the business is in a sector with an extremely high level of competition, then it's not terribly realistic to expect that some run-of-the-mill company will just start taking over the sector and succeed at the rate at which you'd like it to. Some, however, are particularly good within their sectors and have very strong plans. Such was the case of HudBay Minerals, which went from a small company with an even smaller micro-cop to a company worth two and a half billion dollars.

This may seem like obvious enough advice, but you'd be extremely surprised by how many investors and traders completely neglect looking into the basics of a company, like how much their shares are actually worth after taking into account shares outstanding or things such as the company's basic structure.

How to Find a Penny Stock Before It Spikes

It is fairly important for a penny stock trader to be able to notice when a stock is spiking. Of course, there is no 100 percent guarantee that will let you know what every single stock will be doing in every single situation (this is the stock market after all), but there are several signals that you can use in order to try and predict when spikes will occur.

The following list includes some ways to find penny stocks before they spike (number 1 is going to sound very familiar):

1. **Do your research**

One big reason why most people fail when trading penny stocks is simply because they don't realize how much research needs to be done or because they are just too lazy to put the time in to do it. A lot of penny stock traders just want someone to simply tell them what they should do. The biggest problem with that scenario is this: the same person who is telling that trader what to do is also probably telling thousands of other traders the exact same information. Thus, all of these other traders will have already moved in on the proposed opportunity, which means that all that will be left is mere scraps. This won't be enough to make a profit and will actually most likely end up causing the investor to take a loss.

So the real question, then, is how to find out the next big news before the masses, right? The answer for doing so is, of course, research. Look up a stock's disclosure and filings. Find out whether or not that stock has had any recent news in those filings. You may be able to find out that a stock is about to spike using whatever news you find.

2. **Bet on a stock's price action**

Many potential investors make the mistake of attempting to predict when a spike is occurring by paying a visit to their chat room of choice to check in with other members to see what stocks they think may be moving or to see how high they think a specific stock is going to go. Other potential investors may buy alerts from a guru of sorts who might tell them when they should buy, according to their predicted spikes.

This is not to say that all chat rooms are bad. Investors have made a lot of money off of tips from people they trust in certain chat rooms. Ultimately, though, chat rooms are just simply a forum for conversation. Instead, you should really bet on a stock's price action. A stock's price action is its chart movement, and that will give you the actual information about any stock. All of the latest news on every site in the world will not be able to tell you when a stock may break out to a new high or if it has crossed its VWAP, but the chart movement of a stock certainly will.

3. Seek out stocks with the potential for breakouts that are reaching new highs

As a penny stock investor, it may behoove you greatly to always keep an eye out for those stocks that may be following this trend. This especially applies to the stocks that are holding the morning high and still up on the day. You do have to exercise some caution here, though. If you happen to see this play out on a Friday afternoon, there is a big potential for a short squeeze being worked into the close at that point.

4. You can piggyback on a stock that has spiked a bit already

Out of these four strategies, this one will certainly take up a lot less of your time than the others. Piggybacking is where an investor finds a stock that's already on its way up. This is really one of the fastest methods of identifying a stock that is about to spike. There are plenty of research tools available online that can help investors find this information. All you need to do is utilize them.

Hopefully, you will put these strategies to use, and they will help you learn how important it is to properly prepare and research before you buy into any stock, penny or otherwise. The majority of penny stock traders decide not to bother with the work it takes to really dig into the SEC filings of a company they may be interested in, much less take the time to attempt to interpret what all of that information will mean as far as the price of the stock moving higher or lower. This is the reason why the majority of penny stock investors will ultimately end up bankrupting their own portfolios - a lack of preparation and research.

There is no need for you to end up with the same fate. While most people may not find research and preparation to be particularly enjoyable undertakings, keep in mind that this book is not claiming to tell you how to get rich quick or how to have the most fun you've ever had; the purpose of this book is to show you how to be successful in trading penny stocks by providing proven rules and methods of seasoned investors and how to be successful in obtaining the financial freedom that you desire. So, what does it take to really be a success in trading penny stocks?

It takes hard work and a lot of determination. Success in trading in penny stocks requires that you, the investor, put in the time and energy that is necessary in order to reap the kind of benefits that you're seeking. Traders who choose not to put in the necessary time and energy will not accomplish the things that you as a dedicated trader will accomplish, and they will never be able to enjoy the financial freedom that you will be able to enjoy - all because they avoided doing what was necessary to succeed. Even though proper planning may not exactly be fun, it is absolutely crucial in order to achieve success when trading penny stocks.

The Payoff Potential in Penny Stocks

Since there is all this risk and hard work involved, you may be wondering why any potential investor in their right mind would be willing to buy into penny stocks. The answer here is simply the volatility. Penny stocks are very much prone to volatility and violent fluctuation. Knowing this, a lot of investors believe in the possibility of lucking out on a certain stock that they think has the ability to jump from a mere $0.09 up to $9 in just a few weeks. While this is certainly not typical, it has actually happened. If you look through enough message boards that are dedicated to investing, then you will definitely be sure to read some success stories where investors talk about how they made a significant amount of money while "playing the pennies."

It is extremely rare to come across a company that can successfully navigate, making the leap from being a penny stock to becoming a power stock, but on the rare occasion that you do find them, those stocks really pay out in a mind-blowing way. Since the numbers in the penny stock world are so volatile and vary so greatly, some very prepared investors have actually seen gains that reached over 1,000 percent in only a few weeks. Of course, the real trick lies in first being able to find a winning stock, which this chapter has hopefully better prepared you to do.

Enjoying this book so far? I'd love it for you to share your thoughts and post a quick review on Amazon!

Chapter 7: Strategies

It's difficult to encapsulate penny stocks into a few "strategies." This isn't some 1990s video game where there's a set way to win a given level, and it's also not some 2019 video game where there are seven different ways to win a level. The hard truth is that there's no such thing as "winning a level" when it comes to penny stocks because penny stock investing is simply just investing in a market. The market will go up and go down, and a win for one is a loss for another, somewhere. There is no market absolution. If you were to invest in the right thing, then sure, maybe you could consider it a win, but what if you sold and the stock continued to rise? Are you now a loser, since you didn't win as well as you could have? If a stock goes down one day, you might consider yourself a loser - but what if it balloons in price the very next day? Are you a winner now?

The truth is that, in many ways, playing the stock market isn't a game, no matter how fun it can be, and because it's not a game, there are no strict win conditions, nor is there even really a way to win, because there's no such thing as winning.

One can, however, do things that appear like winning. You can develop tendencies that will allow you to generally make the right decision, even if you don't ride a stock all the way to the top or even if things go awry and you have to watch it crash to the bottom.

You can also develop a deep enough knowledge of not only investing but also of the various industries in which you'd like to invest, such that you can make wiser investment choices. However, to say there's a single investment strategy to win every time is silly, because it dilutes the multi-faceted and beautifully enthralling world of finance and trading into a simple dichotomy of winning and losing, which is false.

With all of that in mind, we will go over some tips. These are strategies to help yourself and to change the way you think so that you can look at the market in a better and more clever way.

So, let's go through these ones by one.

1. Examine the waves

The first tip is to watch how the market moves. A ton of studies on penny stocks and penny stock trading have shown that looking at the market with a short-term eye and trading in the short-term is far less risky than trying to trade in the long-term. This is understandable, too. Companies that tend to be based on the penny stock exchanges generally have one of two business models: they are either a new small business with a strong management team and a great product that just need some capital investment in order to get themselves off of the ground or a low-profit small-scale operating company that isn't yielding too much of a result one way or the other.

By recognizing this and trying to trade in the short-term rather than the long-term, you can mitigate the risk that you accidentally invested in the latter rather than the former. Of course, this also should go hand in hand with doing a lot of research on a company and being certain that they're reputable and strong enough to be worth making an investment. However, working in the short-term in combination with a fair amount of research can make a huge difference and make the risky game of penny stocks just a little bit less risky.

So, how do you play in the short term? You play the day trading game of buying low and selling high. It's normal for stocks to be a bit like an ocean wave and fluctuate, going from low to high and back. This is just the life cycle of a stock and is not out of the ordinary whatsoever. When it's in a low, you buy. When it's high, you sell. If you do this with a company that you know well, you can make quite a bit of money.

2. Block out others

I don't mean you should quit listening to your family or feeding your dog. Rather, new investors tend to be highly affected by malicious companies who opt to artificially make their stock more valuable than it actually is. This can be tragic for other investors, but great for the businesses in question. After they've gotten a bunch of new and inexperienced investors to invest in a stock for little to no reason other than word-of-mouth and the fact that they said the stock was a good investment, the owners of the company that spread the word about the stock will then sell their shares in order to make an easy profit.

This problem is becoming even more prevalent now that penny stocks have started to be placed in the spotlight more than they were before. Now, there is technology everywhere and constant communication between people. Penny stocks are no longer relegated to over-the-counter exchanges. Much like options, the fact that we've entered into an information age where people can spread their success stories has led to a lot of interest in penny stocks that weren't there before. Of course, this is exacerbated greatly by the fact that penny stocks are very cheap. This makes them rather appealing to people who aren't wealthy and those who would just like to weekend trade. These people normally play the penny stock exchanges like a lottery, putting their money where they think it should vaguely go and not thinking much more about it. They'll come back to it the following weekend and see just how well their investment went. These kinds of gullible hopeful investors have created a perfect audience for greedy and malicious people out in the real world who think it would be perfectly hilarious to find unsuspecting people and con them into investing in a worthless company so that they can earn a quick buck.

This sort of scam is called a "pump and dump," and it's highly illegal. There are a number of different times in history where pump and dump scams have been all over the news and have been major silver bullets to the ever-fragile world economy. Perhaps the most well-known example of this scam is the Enron debacle.

Back in 2001, a company called Enron was one of America's largest electric and gas companies of all time. The executives at Enron decided that they would craft up a lofty scheme that would make them a ton of money, part of which involved a pump and dump. The scheme was so brilliantly devised that even the most clever and experienced Wall Street financial analysts were tricked. The company was going under for various reasons and was quite in debt. The debt was highly covered up by mark-to-market accounting, which is a form of accounting that aims to present balance sheets and company yields not as they actually are, but as the investors and the stock market would like them to be. The Enron executives were reporting profits high enough in order to inflate the price of Enron's stock, and shortly before the company went bankrupt, nearly thirty Enron executives would sell the stock they had for over a billion dollars altogether. They made a hefty profit, obviously. However, the resulting trial would end up landing most of them behind bars.

Another more fun example of this is Jonathan Lebed's pump and dump scheme. Then only fifteen, he was determined to prove how simple it was to use the internet in order to pull off a successful pump and dump scam. He bought many shares of penny stocks and then went on to promote them on message boards and chat rooms. He pointed at the price increase and told people to buy the stocks that he bought, saying that they were good investments; however, they were not, which was unknown to the people who were falling victim to Lebed's scam! He would then sell his shares for a profit, leaving the stock rather worthless and with the other investors losing a lot of money. It was at this point that the young Lebed landed in the eyes of the SEC. The SEC filed a suit against him. He would not end up going to jail, and instead simply paid back some of his gains and made a promise not to manipulate the markets anymore. At the end of the day, he still walked away with hundreds of thousands of dollars - not half bad for a fifteen-year-old, if you ask me. The young Lebed was very clever, but what he did was highly illegal.

These are just two examples, and the first one shows that you don't necessarily have to be gullible to think that a stock is valuable when it isn't - pretty much the whole of the US investing core thought that Enron was far more valuable than it really was. However, if you keep your wits about you and pay close attention to everything that you're investing in, carefully going over the history of everything that you want to work with, it's highly likely that you can avoid being a money-losing victim in the scheme of someone like Jonathan Lebed.

3. Don't expect too much

One of the reasons you probably even picked up this book was because, at some point, you heard somebody say how much of an untapped gold mine penny stocks are. I'm sure that now, you're a little disenchanted with that concept, especially after reading about all of the risks and scams that happen with penny stock trading. However, maybe there's a part of you that's thinking that you can make a ton of money with penny stocks if you do it correctly. That part of you isn't wrong. In fact, it's technically right.

You can make a bunch of money pushing penny stocks, just like your son can make $50 per day by opening a lemonade stand, or your dog could just relax on the couch when you get home from work instead of jumping on you excitedly. It could happen, but that doesn't mean that it's likely to.

This brings us back to the whole part about respecting the market, and there not being winners and losers. The best investors aren't the ones who make $500,000 off of a single trade. No, those are the luckiest investors. The lucky ones are always winners, but the winners aren't always lucky. You don't have to be lucky to be a good investor.

If you try to coast by on luck alone and you do end up making $500,000 on a single trade, you might decide that it played out really well, and so you must be a master investor. Then, you decide to invest $100,000 of the $500,000 you made in profit back into the penny stock market. You choose to invest in a stock which is rising, and it keeps rising, and you don't sell, and then it takes a nosedive. Maybe the owner of the company got caught in a terrible scandal, or they had a major disaster at one of their main facilities. The stock that you bought is now worth less than what you bought it for, and you've effectively lost a few thousand dollars. So, what happened? Well, you didn't play it risky. Instead of setting a minimum and maximum amount that you'd be happy with, you got greedy and waited for a guarantee of gain that wasn't there. Instead of making back 125 to 150 percent of what you invested, you've now lost about 10 percent.

It's a bit of an extreme example, but it happens on a micro-scale every single day. This is even more important in a market such as penny stock exchanges where everything is so volatile and moving from here to there and back again on a daily basis. If you go in expecting the world, you're going to be intensely disappointed and probably will end up being one of the majority of penny stock investors who end up losing money in the process of investing.

Be happy with little bits here and there. Don't get greedy. If you get lucky, then that's fantastic, but don't rely on luck alone. Build up good trading habits now so that you have them when things do get a little rough.

4. Have a plan

This tip is understated. It's always smart to have a plan no matter what you're doing. However, it's especially important to have a plan in something so volatile as penny stocks.

Now, it may be a little difficult to imagine having a plan when you're working with these stocks. After all, everything is so erratic all the time, so how can one possibly have a plan?

Well, the fact that it's so volatile means that it's especially important to have one. You always need to have a maximum that you'll be happy to gain, a maximum that you'll be happy to lose, and most importantly, an exit plan.

You need a maximum that you'll be happy to gain so that you don't sit down greedily on a stock when something is going your way. You could easily end up losing money this way - possibly more than you're really willing to lose.

You need a maximum that you'll be happy to lose because you don't want to sit around waiting for the stock coming through the tunnel when it may never do so. If a penny stock loses $0.13, of course, it's hypothetically possible in a volatile market that it could make an utter swing and come out the other side and gain back its value really quickly, in the end making you a profit. Of course, it's possible, but that doesn't mean that it's smart to wait around for this to happen, because it may not. Then, if it doesn't, suddenly the negative $0.13 shares you're sitting on are negative $0.25, and you've lost a ton of money. Is that really something that you want to happen?

You always need an exit plan. Have an idea of what you're going to do when the stock is within the boundaries that you've set, whether it's going in your favor or not. Are you going to sell it and sit on the money, or are you going to reinvest it? If so, do you need to be researching other penny stocks you may be interested in? This isn't as vital for securities as it is for futures, but it's still worthwhile to have an exit plan for your timing and your events afterward. Even one personally stagnant moment in the world of finance can make all the difference.

5. Don't let your emotions get in the way

This tip is arguably the most important. You absolutely cannot let your emotions get in the way. What do I mean by emotions? I mean greed, anger, sadness, vindication, happiness, etc. When you're in front of your stock portfolio or your trading platform, all that you should allow yourself to think in are rational absolutes. Anything that isn't a rational absolute isn't worth your time and will only throw you off course.

You may be wondering what is exactly implied by letting your emotions get in the way. Let's say that you suffer a loss on a stock, and so to make up for that loss, you end up pouring even more money into the next investment that you make with the rationale that a profit on that will make up for both the losses and the disappointments of the prior failed trade. You decide to invest in another stock in a rush, only barely looking at the stock's history and the company itself.

Is that rational at all? No, of course not. However, you'd be surprised by how often this happens to people who'd like to be financial traders.

Money isn't an art, but rather a science. Spare your emotions for art. Money is a game of math. The answers to your high school algebra assignments weren't allowed to change depending upon whether you felt happy, sad, or angry on any given day, so why would you allow the way you handle your money to change with your emotions? The basic operations don't change, as they shouldn't, so why would anything else change? That's absurd. Money is money is money, and it is absolute, so treat it absolutely, as you would math or chemistry.

So, what exactly can you do to avoid letting your emotions get in the way? Well, having your investing money detached from the money you need to live can help, hence why earlier in the book, it was recommended that you only use speculative investing money that you can spare in order to invest in penny stocks. Using anything else is not only risky but a wholly bad idea. You need money to get by in life. Therefore, don't make the stupid mistake of mixing your gambling money with your energy bill. That's how you lose your lights, and believe me, you don't want to lose your lights.

Don't forget to take time to decompress each day and get away from your investments. Designate part of your day to meditate and possibly practice the tenets of Zen if you're so inclined. Give yourself a massage to release your tension, or set up a very comfortable couch in front of a bright window and take time each day to sit in front of it and bask in the light, revitalizing yourself and calming your nerves, which are surely on edge from a long day of trading and market unpredictability.

Do whatever you can in order to be certain that you yourself are healthy because your wellness always comes first. When your body and mind are healthy and relaxed, clear decision-making will follow.

6. Keep a journal

This is a big one. Keep a record of your trading patterns, both good and bad. Record your thoughts on each trade and how those trades go for you. If something stuck out to you about a company, record that. Do whatever you can in order to document your thought process when you're trading.

Why should you do this? Well, there's hardly anybody better to learn from than yourself. I can guarantee that some of the greatest lessons you'll ever learn are from your own mistakes (and also the mistakes of others, of course). Learn what things go wrong for you, and try to keep up with your own head in terms of what you're thinking (or what you aren't thinking) when you make the good (or bad) decisions that you do.

You'll eventually develop your own style of trading, and this will help you to find out what works best for you. Maybe you find that you're actually rather good at seeking out companies that will be good in the long-term, and your strength is to invest more in the companies that you think will do well. On the other hand, maybe you'll figure out that when you invest a lot, you don't do as well. This might tell you that you need to make smaller investitures and diversify more. Everyone has a different temperament and a different way of thinking about things. By studying your own thoughts and your own tendencies - how much you invest, when you invest, the way in which you invest, whether you take profits or losses - will teach you a lot about the game of trading and about your own way of playing it.

You won't always make the right decisions. In fact, a lot of the time, you won't. That's where this journal will come in handy.

Dollar Cost Averaging (DCA)

Numerous investors, especially the ones who are just starting to invest, are under the wrong impression that in order to gain a high profit in trading, they have to buy and sell shares at the same time. Of course, this strategy can prove useful if you don't want to hire a broker and want to save money by limiting or eliminating broker commission fees. However, you'll find that the advantages are fewer ('Trading Strategy,' 2019).

A better strategy that is proven to work is DCA. As you should know by now, penny stocks tend to be very unpredictable and volatile. You should always avoid the short-term upsides and downsides that a lot of penny stocks have. As an investor, you can benefit by using Dollar-Cost Averaging. The simple process of the DCA strategy is as follows: purchase additional shares of the stock at precise and pre-established set intervals (no matter the activity of the share price) rather than purchasing all the shares at the same time.

Usually, with the DCA, many people buy shares when the stock price is low, and they don't when the stock price is high. Using the DCA strategy, however, you will lower the risk of investing a large amount of money into a single investment that can turn out to be bad and reap negative returns. The average price will be lower than what it would be if you purchased all the shares at a price peak. Overall, keep in mind that you should absolutely avoid the high risk that comes with purchasing a large number of shares when the stock price is at its highest. Invest in small intervals over an extended period of time instead.

There is, however, a downside to the DCA. This relates to the commission you must pay to the broker; every transaction requires a new commission to be paid. Nonetheless, the positives of DCA win over the negatives, because minimizing risk is probably the most important thing, and it cannot (and should not) be compared to a commission cost.

Reverse Mergers

Do an advanced search for penny stocks that match your investment and trading criteria, looking for public stocks that have gained their status through a "reverse merger."

Here is what happens in a reverse merger: a public company that possesses a small or nonexistent amount of assets merges with a private company that not only has assets but also has operations and personnel. When the successful, private company merges with the struggling public company, it becomes publicly traded. If you own stock in a private company and want to make it public, this is a very easy way to do so.

Let's use an example to better clarify this point. We are going to use the private company ABC that has $5 million of earnings and wishes to go public. ABC contacts a small company that agrees to give them a major part of their stock, and in return, the small company will own a small stake in ABC. The public company obtains ABC for around $0.10 a share. After the merger is finished, the reverse-merged company makes a press release stating that the private company went public, that their management team is still the same, and that the company underwent a beneficial and successful merger.

If ABC keeps growing, stocks will move even higher in price since there are many investors interested in buying shares of merged companies. This may not always be the case, however. Sometimes companies that undergo a reverse-merger don't see a profitable rise in their stock prices. In essence, it all depends on the newly created public company; if that company fails, the stock prices will encounter a decline, which will lead to a loss of money for the investors.

Stop-Loss Orders

Stop-losses are something every investor or trader needs to know how and when to manage. They are sell orders that are triggered if the stock or stocks purchased fall any percentage below the original purchase price. Stop-loss orders will save you from financial hardships that occur when shares experience frequent declines. There are two different subcategories of stop-loss orders: automatic and mental. What category you find yourself and your investments under will depend upon your broker; some brokers will let you set up an automatic stop-loss order, while other brokers need to do it manually.

Below we have detailed how both an automatic and mental stop-loss order work:

- **Automatic:** If you are allowed to set up an automatic stop-loss order on a couple of penny stocks, your stock will be put on sale once it reaches your pre-established "stop" price. If this option is available, use it. These are more reliable than the mental.

- **Mental:** With this one, you already have a trigger price in mind. You sell when shares fall below your pre-established price, but this selling is done manually by your broker. There's no system in place to sell your share automatically, hence the difference between automatic and mental stop-loss. However, when you purchase a stock using mental stop-loss, don't forget to set up a price alert at the level you decide to stop at so you aren't caught off guard if and when the time comes.

One of the hardest elements about investing is selling your shares when they hit the mental stop-loss level. Many investors try to either find a way out of the position or keep their investments. If you want to use stop-loss orders successfully as an investment strategy, then stick with it and don't ask questions or make excuses. Like any other strategy, stop-losses are not free of risk. One of the biggest risks that hide among penny stock trading and investing is the possibility of being stopped out. This is referred to as a "fall price swing." This is when you hit your pre-established stop-loss price, and soon afterward, you sell the stock, only to observe the price of shares in that same penny stock go up once again.

If you find yourself entering a situation like this, there are a few things you can do to prevent yourself from getting completely stopped out:

- **Set stop-losses on high trading volume shares** - These penny stocks will have less price volatility in general. Once the stock starts falling, a lot of the observing investors may buy at the lower prices and thus push the shares high once again.

- **Use stop-loss on penny stocks that have a low volatility history** - If a penny stock currently has high volatility, you can count on it to only increase in the future. The lower the volatility, the better the chances of not being stopped out on price swings.

- **Set up stop-loss on stocks for which you expect a great price decline** - Instead of setting your stop level at 5 or 10 percent below your buying price, think about dropping it down to 25 percent of your original purchase price. This lower stop may put you at financial risk, but it will also lower the risk of getting stopped out if there is a brief fall in shares. You'll need to determine what your personal preferences are and what you think works best in your unique financial situation when following this suggestion.

- **Purchase shares on price dips** - Wait and purchase stock shares after a price dip. This will lead to short-term upsides and won't fall too much in the future. When you purchase penny stocks after they experience price dips, you lower your chance of getting stopped out in the near future.

Position Sizing

Position sizing is probably the best strategy for keeping your portfolio safe, yet it's somehow misunderstood by all too many investors, experienced and inexperienced. With position sizing, you are limiting every purchase to an already determined percentage of your own portfolio. So, for example, let's say you have a $10,000 portfolio and you choose to limit your biggest purchase to $500. This will be roughly 5 percent of your portfolio. Yes, with this strategy, you are certainly limiting your profit opportunities, but you are also protecting your investments from a downfall. This strategy is appropriate for bigger portfolios. If you are a trader with a $240,000 portfolio, for example, you may benefit by purchasing stocks worth $4,000, which means that you'll be able to purchase around 60 different stocks. Doing so will risk just a small part of your portfolio on every single stock. If your portfolio is small, it may not work out in the best way possible with this strategy. If you have only $3,000 to invest, it would be pointless to divide this relatively small amount among 10 penny stocks.

When to Take and When to Sell a Profit

There are highly effective strategies that will help you determine the perfect time to withdraw your profit and when you should sell your stock if the price experiences a gradual and/or steady decline.

- **Stopping at a profit** - If you invested in a stock and its price has risen significantly from the price you bought it at, it would be a safe and profitable investment move to sell and take the profit while you can. Doing so locks in your gains. When shares are trading at a significantly higher price than your purchase price, you should lock in your gains instead of taking financial risks. If the stock looks unfavorable, and financial analysis shows that the company may soon experience a decline, you should absolutely consider taking your profit before any major financial changes occur. Even if you are wrong and the price of the stock goes up, you can rest assured that you've still made a considerable profit and have the funds to pursue further investment opportunities. If there is no loss, you experience no stress.

- **Take your losses** - You'll need to learn to accept your losses when they happen, which means accepting your financial mistakes, learning from them, and moving forward. As already mentioned, selling shares at a loss is probably the hardest thing you are going to stumble upon as an investor. Penny stocks are risky by nature, which means that you should always know what happens concerning the company you are investing in, and if their stock price declines.

Moving Averages (MA)

Moving averages can be very helpful when it comes to penny stocks because they can identify clear buying and selling signals. Moving averages can be described as the average price of your shares over a selected time frame. For example, a seven-day MA will display the average price of stock each day, with the seventh day included. In general, if you have a couple of MAs, they will be applied at the same time, which makes your trades very clear.

The moving averages are looking back, which means that they display the changes in the prices until this point rather than making predictions regarding what the shares will do when they keep moving forward. You'll be able to spot the beginning of a trade if you notice some momentum price changes of a stock, which will be portrayed by moving average lines of crossing lengths that have different timing. The strategy in this technical analysis indicator is when shares start to go up or down significantly, the new prices should outpace the MA that is lagging.

You can see this outpace by the moving average breaking away from the shares price. When a major trend starts, the price of the share will begin to move higher. Afterward, throughout the following days, there will be a movement up in the shorter moving average. In the end, the longer MA will start going up, and the shorter MA will lag. As an investor, you should know a few things about the moving averages:

- **Time length** - If you want to use moving averages successfully, you should select their duration. Rather than looking for the best and most effective duration, you should find the one that will be the most reliable. If you pick a short MA time frame, the prices should be more responsive at the beginning, because in order to calculate the average, a few days will be needed.

- **The number of moving average** - Many TAs involve two moving averages. Of course, there are investors who prefer to use only one, but others think it's more beneficial to use three or more MA lines. If you're investing in penny stocks, in particular, the most effective way to do so is to use exactly two MA lines.

- **Buy and sell signals** - Every time a short MA crosses a long one, it indicates a buy signal. When the MA indicators display the trending up of the short-term prices, this means a stock uptrend. On the other hand, when the short MA goes below the long one, it implies a sell. When the MA indicator displays that the short-term prices are going beneath the long-term average price, this indicates a stock downtrend.

The key to being a successful trader and investor relies upon the strategies you understand and embrace during your time in the stock market.

Chapter 8: Risk Management

Since they are typically issued by small and growing companies with limited resources as well as limited cash, and because their shares are considered to be extremely speculative, penny stocks are known for being very volatile and more suited for those investors who have a high-risk tolerance. All in all, the majority of penny stocks tend to have low trading volumes and also tend to be high-risk investments. As an investor, there are some things that you need to be aware of, including some of the risks that are involved with trading penny stocks. Keep in mind that penny stocks have earned every bit of their bad reputation, but educating yourself will remove a lot of the extra risk involved.

The Risks Associated with Penny Stocks

Aside from the usual risks that come with trading volatile stocks, here are some things that you may not be aware of, even if you're not a total beginner:

- Spam - everyone has seen it, and everyone despises it. As an investor, spam can be found not only in the inbox of your email but also through many places online. Penny stocks are not immune, either. Scammers make a lot of money by promoting sketchy penny stocks to investors that may not know that this practice exists.

- Be aware of dilution. Sometimes a company will need to issue additional stock in order to gain capital. When this happens, it usually leads to the dilution of the stock that's already held by its investors, meaning that the stock decreases in value. This is commonplace and is not considered to be shady dealings at all, but it's certainly something that investors need to be aware of.

- Pink sheets and the OTCBB do not have to meet minimum standard requirements to stay on the exchange. Minimum standards are in place to protect investors and as a guideline for companies issuing stock. When first starting out, you may want to stick with trading on a major exchange, because they have regulations in place which protect you and your investment.

- The short squeeze is a tricky, calculated situation where a very heavily shorted commodity or stock moves higher very sharply and forces the short sellers to close out their short positions, which only adds to the stock's sudden upward pressure. The term "short squeeze" refers to the fact that the short sellers are effectively being "squeezed" out of their position in the stock, and they typically find themselves at a loss.

- One issue penny stocks are known for is the difficulty in finding necessary information and history about them, which makes it even more difficult to form an educated decision when trading (Staff, 2016). If you paid enough attention to what worked for you and what didn't when you were paper trading and heeded the warnings and advice of trusted sources such as this book, you should be able to make more informed decisions.

- Penny stocks are known for not having much liquidity. This means that it can be really difficult to sell a stock once you have bought it, and you may have to lower your price below your buying price in order for that stock to sell. Low liquidity in a stock also makes it more vulnerable to manipulation and pump and dump type scams.

- The pump and dump scam is probably the most common scam associated with penny stocks, so you need to keep your eyes open and know what to look for. The pump and dump consist of a worthless stock being bought up by an individual or company. Then, the worthless stock is hyped up, and investors who are inexperienced end up buying these worthless stocks at a heightened price - this is the pump.

When the inexperienced investors have bought enough of the stock to drive the price up enough, the person or company who initially bought the previously worthless stock then sells all of their shares, which effectively makes the stock worthless again. This is known as the dump. Beware!

10 Ways to Protect Yourself and Prepare for Financial Freedom

Some investors may not be aware of the methods that are available for protecting themselves when investing in penny stocks and can end up getting burned or losing all of their hard earned savings. There is some repeated information made in the following list of pointers that can be found in other parts of this book, but just know that this repetition serves a purpose. Some things just bear repeating. Be mindful of the following points in order to avoid the scams, misleading information, and low-quality investments associated with penny stock investment:

1. **Prepare yourself by doing your research**. Anyone who has ever invested in penny stocks will tell you that you need to prepare and research as much as possible before you buy in. You don't anticipate winding up as one of those super sad statistics where you lose everything

because you got bamboozled. Have you ever wondered why Wall Street is always profiting, no matter what? Wall Street always profits, because there is always someone buying into stocks which have not done their research and, therefore, loses their money. So make sure to do your research.

2. **If you come across a penny stock tip in your email or on social media, just say no.** Do not spend any time at all on these types of tips. Many inexperienced investors buy up these stocks like they're lotto tickets when the jackpot is up to hundreds of millions of dollars. That definitely isn't the right way to handle these tips; just ignore them altogether.

3. **Read the disclaimers on all penny stock newsletters.** In general, penny stocks are sold more than they are bought. A huge contributor to this fact is the misinformation contained in those newsletters that convince potential investors to buy and buy quickly. Keep in mind that penny stock newsletters do not dole out free advice just to be nice. The disclaimers at the bottom of these newsletters will inform you whether or not someone is just trying to create hype by making a false promise about their worthless companies.

4. **Never listen to what a company's management says about their stock.** This closely correlates with the previous point on

the grounds that, yet again, someone is trying to manipulate you as the investor into purchasing what will be a scam. Most penny stocks are actually thought to be scams themselves. They are stocks that are built up by a company so that they can stay in business and created with the sole purpose of enriching only the business' insiders by taking advantage of investors. Be aware that there is a large group of people who run penny stock promotions using all kinds of different press releases (think newsletters, social media, etc.) and different companies. In fact, one of these people has actually recently returned to the stock market after being convicted of a pump and dump scam while barely in high school.

5. **Be quick to sell.** After all of the unnerving information above, the good news is that it is possible to make 20 or 30 percent of your penny stocks in just a few days. This is the main reason why people are drawn to them. When you happen to see this kind of return, you need to put your curiosity or greed aside and sell immediately; this is because penny stocks can be so volatile that you never know when the 20 or 30 percent may suddenly drop to nothing at all. In penny stocks, it is not very prudent to hold out for a 1,000 percent return. Take your profits and move on.

6. **Do not trade big.** Trading big is also known

as trading large positions, and you need to be really careful about your position sizing when it comes to penny stocks. As a rule of thumb, it is smart not to trade more than about 10 percent of a stock's daily volume. You'll actually want to limit your share size so that it will be easier for you to sell the stock more quickly, which ultimately results in making more money.

7. **Only focus on those penny stocks that have a high volume.** Try to deal with penny stocks that trade a minimum of 100,000 shares per day. Penny stocks with lower volumes are more difficult to sell, and so they're also more difficult to make money on.

8. **Give yourself limits and guidelines.** Learn what risk-reward ratios work for you and stick to them when buying and selling your penny stock shares. While there may be a time or two that you could have made more money if you would have waited for just a little longer, sticking to the limits you create for yourself will end up generating more profit for you in the long run.

9. **Do not get attached to any penny stock because someone tells you to be.** This can be especially difficult to do when a family member or a friend specifically recommends a particular stock and are very enthusiastic about its potential. Also, each and every penny stock company out there would love for you to think

that it has the most potentially profitable stock with the most exciting story and that it will revolutionize the known world. As you are entering the arena of penny stock trading, it is extremely wise to be very cynical, to diversify, and to rely on your own research (there's that word, again) before you buy into any penny stock.

10. **Look for the penny stocks that are having an earnings breakout.** A stock that has good earnings will be breaking out to 52-week highs and will be trading at a volume of at least 250,000 shares per day. If you know where and how to look, these types of penny stocks can be relatively easy to find. However, the challenge comes again in avoiding a pump and dump scam that is behind the 52-week highs of a penny stock.

Chapter 9: Identifying Good Companies

At the heart of all of the metrics and ratios is the search for a good company. As a penny stock investor, all you're really looking for at the end of the day is a business that knows what it's doing and one that just so happens to have cheap stock at the moment. You're looking for a company that's having success serving a market, that's able to grow, and is run by competent people (Lewis, 2019).

Look for Companies Matching a Strong Angle with Financial Competence

The previous chapter listed a multitude of metrics that can help shed light on a business's ability to attain the financial goals it needs to, but if you're looking to invest in a company that's going to succeed big, then you have to make sure that the business itself is clearly viable and that it has a great angle. This type of information about a business can be found in press releases, internet chat rooms, on the company's website, and in the media. Below is a fictional account of what your research process may look like.

Let's say you get a tip in a chat room or on a penny stock investor website that a certain stock trading at $5 per share has great potential. Let's say that the stock is Wellness Express (WEX). According to your source, Wellness Express was set up in the United States to open a string of healthy, quick-service restaurants in small-to-medium-sized towns. They offer a selection of pre-prepared healthy dishes as well as a made-to-order menu to deliver healthy and fast meal options to their patrons. Their angle is that people will choose to pursue healthy eating options on-the-go when those options are presented to them in a convenient way, and they are more comfortable getting food in a small store environment than they are in a large supermarket where they face a busy parking lot, potentially heavy foot traffic, a long checkout line, and limited sit-down space.

The concept resonates with you as a reasonable business angle, so you jump on your broker's website or the website for the exchange where WEX is being traded and check out its numbers. WEX has a quick ratio of 1.3 and an operating cash flow ratio of 0.8, which is not bad from a liquidity standpoint. The company is making sales at $11.50 for every share; that's a price-to-sales ratio of 11.50 to 5, which is indicative of a company that's reaching its market. The price-to-book ratio is just above 1, so you know that the current stock price of $5 is low. Maybe you've found your diamond for the day, so you buy.

Since there are tens of thousands of penny stocks from which to choose, you can't crunch the numbers for all of them.

Note: *Some software programs allow you to filter penny stocks by various markets, ratios, and prices. So, if you want to look at a list of all stocks selling at less than $4 per share with a price-to-book ratio of at least 1 and a quick ratio of 1 or higher, then you can set those parameters in your software and generate a list.*

You have to be able to supplement your quantitative

analysis with a qualitative one. You can do this by inspecting the company's image. Has it put any work toward branding? With the fictitious health foods company, WEX, it would be worth a look at the company website and menu. You could also use Google Maps to take a street-view look at where the restaurants are being placed. Does the area look well-trafficked? Does the sign and façade of the restaurant look attractive? Is the restaurant logo and color scheme attractive?

Branding is especially important with penny stock companies because they are usually in the process of introducing themselves to the market and making a case as to why they deserve market share. In the case of WEX, the company is trying to persuade the market that it's possible to eat healthy on-the-go. Therefore, customers must see Wellness Express as a credible source of good food. Below are some ways for an investor to tell when a company is leveraging good branding toward the promotion of a good business.

The company provides relentless value at every interaction point.

A company that's well branded and destined to survive and thrive aggressively delivers value to the consumer at every opportunity. The company should have a website that's easy to use, be ready to add new visitors to their mailing list and give direction to their stores. These may all seem like common sense concerns, but if a company has invested in creating and hosting a website, then it should be maximizing its utility with every customer visit.

The company stands out from the crowd.

A company destined to succeed must have a sense of inspiration about it. It must be distinct from other retailers in its space. In the case of WEX, the company defines itself as a fast food alternative: get the speed and convenience of fast food without the nutritional drawbacks.

The company cultivates focus in its branding.

A company that's going to thrive in its market must be clearly focused on its mission and dedicated to serving a specific market sector. One thing that often leads smaller companies to fail or stagnate is over-diversifying or switching course too frequently. If WEX purports itself to deliver healthy food fast, then it doesn't also offer authentic Chinese food, the best coffee in town, or even the best tasting veggie burger on the market. In reality, there's no reason that WEX can't offer all of these things. In fact, it would be great if it did. But when it comes to the branding of the company, it must remain steady and focused on one particular market entry point.

The company communicates well.

When a company is eager to communicate with its customers via emails, surveys, focus groups, or the like, and also communicates with its investors via reports or press releases, then the company is clearly committed to its own success. That's an important commitment, seeing as not all companies you'll encounter, especially in the penny stock trade, are going to maintain their passion. Look for companies that aggressively seek feedback and new insight into the market they're trying to reach.

The company cultivates its own distinct and consistent style.

A company that's poised to grow is a company with a very clear and consistent vision for itself. This is perhaps the most important qualitative attribute that you can look for in a winning investment, but perhaps also the most difficult attribute to put into words. A company often comes into its own long before it financially matures. This is that rare, elusive point at which the savviest investors have a real opportunity to reap dramatically high returns on a penny stock investment. The key is consistency in branding.

Look for evidence that the company has secured some kind of essential image for itself that creates sparks of eminence and inevitability. These abstract elements can be manifested in a variety of ways. In our WEX example, perhaps the investor notices a rich consistency of branding across the company's in-store experience, its online branding, and its email marketing styles, such as the same colors, the same voice, the same feel, or a sense of a new entity being born and to great purpose. This is where investing, penny stock or otherwise, becomes much more of an art than a science.

The Penny Stock Branding Advantage

One advantage that a smaller, lesser-known, or unknown company has over a larger, established company is the ability to flexibly position its brand. Keeping with the example, let's say that Whole Foods saw the need for a healthy meal-on-the-go option in medium-sized cities. Because it already has a reputation for being a higher-end grocery store, it would face an uphill branding battle if it tried to compete with the smaller and newer Wellness Express. Why? Because Wellness Express has cultivated focus around its branding. Wellness Express is about one thing and one thing only: providing diners with great healthy food. Not to say that Whole Foods couldn't eventually position itself to be a viable option for this market need, but it would require a lot more effort on the part of Whole Foods. The company would have to readjust its floor plan a bit to allow for an expansion of its dining area, and it would need to open a separate checkout station so that diners would be able to check out quickly and eat while their food was still hot. Speaking of hot food, extra care would need to be taken with the preparation and sale of hot food items, since more of these items would be consumed on site, rather than taken home where they could be reheated and microwaved.

Perform Technical and Fundamental Analyses before Buying

"Fundamental analysis" and "technical analysis" are two terms that get thrown around a lot in the investment world. Fundamental analysis refers to drilling down on the essentials that make a company tick. Who sits on the board of directors, who's managing the company, what is communicated by the company's press releases, and how does this company fare within its industry? Technical analysis refers to looking at all the charts and graphs and other goodies showing how the stock's price has changed over time, its trading volume, and other facts that provide give an indication of what the company's future share value will look like. The methods you use largely depend on the type of investor you are - some call this your "investor personality" - and whether you feel more comfortable betting on trends and data or solid people and a good story.

The Typical Penny Stock

One potential problem with the WEX (Wellness Express) example is that we're envisioning a penny stock that, presumably, already has an active retail location and is generating a substantial cash flow. As a penny stock investor, you're more likely to be confronted with companies that are still in the early research and development phases, approaching some untested market with a new concept, and no one knows whether or not it's going to work. You'll also find everything in between. You'll have a lot of options to choose from, so you will need to whittle down your choices some. Below are some ways you can do this.

Trade in market sectors that you know - Being a successful penny stock investor requires a lot of dedicated research time. It's not always fun. Focusing on market sectors in which you're genuinely interested makes it easier for you to stay up-to-date and intrigued. By being an expert in a given area and investing in companies and sectors you understand, you'll be different from most investors who follow the media buzz and move with the swarm from sector to sector, chasing whatever the pundits happen to say is "hot" at the time.

Note: *The prices of these media-hyped stocks tend to overinflate and then plummet, and many investors suffer losses. Many stock "experts" print off weekly tip sheets, purportedly telling them where to find the hottest penny stocks. More often than not, the hype results in the stock trading for more money than it's really worth. Its poor fundamentals eventually betray it, and it again plummets in value. So, how do you weather the waves of hype? It's simple - learn how to conduct sound fundamental and technical analyses of the stocks you're interested in purchasing.*

Look for critical pre-market success indicators - Depending on the industry, various fundamental factors determine how strong a stock is before its product or service even goes to market. For example, if the company is based on producing and marketing a new invention, then you should check to see that the company has acquired a 10-year patent on the invention. If they haven't received their patent yet, check to see if they're working on improving their product to a point at which patenting is possible. If the company is a bank, a consultancy, or a research group, then inspect the existing and pending relationships. Does the company have financing from a solid source? Does it have sufficient financing to stay afloat for at least 12 more months? Does it have the right partners in place to meet its marketing needs, such as advertisers and agents? Is there any government involvement in the company? Has the company applied for a grant or entered into a dialog with a government entity regarding the future purchase of the company's products? Did it get little more than token attention from these entities, or did it really captivate them?

Make sure the company's debt is serviceable - It's not uncommon for penny stocks to have debts that exceed their assets. Nonetheless, if the company has incurred debt that's over three times the value of its assets, then it's in a very vulnerable financial position.

How and When to Cash In

Investment in penny stocks is quite different from traditional stock investment, largely because of all the strange but potent hype that surrounds them. Because the stock price is so volatile, a little bit of good press can send the price soaring. These media pumps don't always work, and the high price rarely sustains itself before going back down. Winning penny stock investors do not buy in the heat of a price-spiking media parade, but are already holding significant shares of the stock at the time the media parade commences.

When you find yourself holding a penny stock that's spiking high, usually, the prudent thing to do is to sell within one hour (and no longer than 3 months) after the initial spike. The reason for this is because, in most cases, the stock eventually plummets back down.

Use the cash you free up to reinvest in other stocks. (Remember, the more you invest, the more experience you gain, and the better your insight and intuition become.) If your exploding penny stock continues to climb higher and higher after you sell, don't fret about it, as this happens. You did the right thing by insulating yourself from undue risk.

Chapter 10: Metrics

This chapter deals with some critical metrics to help you make better decisions when choosing penny stocks (Leeds, 2018). Every good investment is essentially built on a story - a reason why the current price for a particular security is lower than it should be. Even though you can't predict the future, the ability to tell a compelling story that forecasts a probable future outcome can be a powerful tool. However, since you're dealing with dollars and cents and profits and loss, you need to incorporate rock hard data into your stories wherever possible.

Penny stocks usually draw a lot of attention from investors, because they're cheap to acquire. Investors who only have a few hundred dollars to throw into the market are drawn to penny stocks, because they can buy a substantial quantity, and, at times, they can realize astronomical gains. You're reading this book because you want to maximize your chances at realizing a great return. You want a strategy to succeed.

Liquidity Ratios

Understanding how to use liquidity ratios insulates you from one of the major hazards of penny stock investing - investing in a company that cannot pay its short-term obligations. Many stocks are priced low, specifically because they are unable to service their debts. You want to steer clear of these stocks, and you can easily do so by learning how to access and interpret these relatively simple ratios, which are detailed below.

Current Ratio - This liquidity ratio is found by dividing a company's current assets by its current liabilities. You're looking for a value of 1 or higher, indicating that the company has enough value in its assets to cover its currently outstanding liabilities. If the ratio is 1/3, then it's in your best interest to stay away from this penny stock. Its debt is three times as large as the value of its current assets. If the ratio, on the other hand, has a value of 3, then you understand that the firm's assets are sufficient to cover its liabilities three times over.

Quick Ratio - The quick ratio is essentially the current ratio with more restrictions placed upon what qualifies as an "asset." The quick ratio defines assets as only cash, accounts receivable, and marketable securities.

The objective of the quick ratio is to give the investor a sense for the value of a company's assets that can be quickly and expediently liquidated. The quick ratio is thought to be more accurate than the current ratio, seeing as some of the assets included in the current ratio may not be truly liquid and may not have the same value when resold. Like the current ratio, the investor should seek a value of 1 or higher to feel at ease with the company's ability to service its short-term debts.

Cash Ratio - Cash is king, and a good cash ratio makes a penny stock investment even safer than just a good quick ratio. The cash ratio is essentially the quick ratio with accounts receivable removed from the calculation. You're left with cash plus marketable securities divided by liabilities. By removing accounts receivable, you no longer need to worry about whether the company's customers are ever going to pay them. Everything they have immediately on hand is accounted for and nothing else. With penny stocks, it's not necessarily a deal breaker if a company has a weaker cash ratio. A value of at least 1 is a good benchmark to ensure that the company will be able to remain in business and service all of its debts due within a year.

Operating Cash Flow Ratio - Operating cash flow is an even stricter measurement of a company's short-term financial solvency. This liquidity ratio is calculated using only the incoming cash from company operations in the numerator and dividing it by the company's current liabilities. In the case of this ratio, it's alright if your value is less than 1, as other liquid assets can be brought in if needed to service the company's debts; however, if the operating cash flow ratio drops too low, then the company may be facing some serious financial trouble. If the operating cash flow is 1 or more, then the company is bringing in enough cash through normal business operations to service its debts for the next 12 months, which is a really good sign for a penny stock.

Note: As a general rule, investors prefer companies that have solid cash flow and the ability to readily cover all of their debts. If you can find a company in this position that's priced cheaply (see Price-to-Book, Price-to-Earnings, and Price-to-Sales below), then you've found a good penny stock prospect.

There are several reasons why a stock's operating cash flow is important. These reasons have been outlined below:

1. If the company has a strong operating cash flow, then it must be bringing in a substantial income, meaning that whatever products or services are being sold are reaching a significant market, and that market is likely to continue creating a real demand.
2. When operational cash flow is heavy, the firm is able to take advantage of growth opportunities. The company may hire new employees, invest in new assets, or purchase back its own stock shares.
3. A company with a strong operational cash flow is less likely to take on more debt. Without the necessity to raise more money, slowing it down, the company is free to focus on further expansions of its business.

Price-to-Book - The price-to-book ratio, or P/B

ratio, is an interesting indicator that can help you determine whether a stock, regardless of its share price, is truly inexpensive. Let's take a look at a fictional penny stock, Brayton Co., or "BYT," that trades for $3. Let's say that BYT is listed on the OTCQX, so you are able to access some decent financial data. To find the stock's P/B ratio, you first need to get its market capitalization (market cap) value, which is listed next to every stock on the OTCQX. Market cap simply refers to the number of outstanding shares multiplied by the share value. Let's say BYT has 3 million outstanding shares and thus has a market cap of $9 million.

Next, you'll need to find the company's "book price." The book price is what the company would be left with after all of its assets were liquidated, and all of its liabilities paid. A company's book price can usually be determined by looking at its most recent balance sheet, which is a listing of all assets and liabilities. Now, let's say that you are able to find BYT's book price and that the company "goes to book" at 12 million dollars. This means that the company is selling at 3/4 of its book value (below book value), which is another way of saying it's inexpensive, or perhaps a good deal.

Note: *Sometimes, P/B ratio is calculated using all per share values. Each share's book value has to be established. In our example, BYT would have a per share book value of 12 million divided by 3 million or a book value per share of $4. The P/B ratio would* *thus be 3/4. You will always get the same P/B value, no matter which calculation method you use. Some investors like to look at per-share book value and compare it to the stock value.*

In theory, the P/B ratio is exceptionally important for penny stocks because the companies that issue penny stocks are more likely to be on the brink of bankruptcy. If a company's share value is lower than its per-share book value, and the company goes bankrupt immediately, then theoretically, the loss would be smaller than it would have been had the share value been higher than the book value. Therefore, investing in companies with a lower P/B ratio can serve as a stop-loss against risky investments.

As with any financial ratio investors use, a company's price-to-book can bode both well and poorly for the company's future stock value. In our example, BYT's stock is selling for less than its per-share book value. Some investors would say that this is an indication that the stock has been underpriced, and, assuming that the company is still fundamentally in good shape and there aren't any unpleasant surprises, the stock should go up in value. So get in now while it's hot. Another investor may look at the stock and think: it's a penny stock; it's likely to go bankrupt, so in the best case the investors will get some of their money back and take a modest loss. This is not so good.

It's important to realize here that a strategy is not following a fail-safe, inflexible plan of operation, but building a knowledge base in order to make informed decisions. This is the classic difference between "strategy" and "tactics." Tactics refer to a clear-cut action plan that, if executed correctly, produces a very specific result; strategy refers to the more artistic pursuit of gently honing the larger picture toward your vision for success. When it comes to investments, calculating a penny stock's P/B ratio is a tactic, and deciding whether or not to buy the stock is a strategy.

Growth Rates

Anyone can easily understand this metric. What does the penny stock's growth history look like? Has the stock been taking a steady plummet over the last several quarters, or is it ascending to great heights with no end in sight?

When assessing a stock's growth pattern, make sure that you're looking at quarterly markers, if not monthly ones. Looking at a stock's growth on a year-by-year basis can be a bit deceptive, as smaller yet meaningful growth changes can occur within the confines of a year. If you only look at growth benchmarks on a year-by-year basis, then you may miss crucial patterns.

Take, for example, a stock that has a market cap value of $25 million in the spring quarter of 2014. It grows to $40 million in the summer quarter, then begins declining to $35 million in the fall quarter and is at $33 million in the winter quarter. In the spring quarter of 2015, it's at $30 million. The market cap value has declined over the last three quarters. As long as you're evaluating the stock in quarterly increments, you will see this. If an investor fails to review the quarterly increments and only evaluates the stock in annual increments, seeing the spring 2014 quarter at $25 million and then the spring 2015 quarter at $30 million, he may mistakenly assume that the stock is on a steady upward trajectory.

The same mistaken evaluation can occur in the inverse. Let's say the stock has a market cap value of $30 million in the spring of 2014 and then slumps to $15 million by the summer of 2014, and then it's at $20 and $23 million, in the fall and winter quarters, respectively. By the spring quarter of 2015, the stock continues its steady ascent to $26 million, but if the investor were looking at the stock on a year-by-year basis, then they would see that it was at $30 million in the spring of 2014 and $26 million in the spring of 2015. Thus, they may assume that the growing stock is actually stagnant.

So, what really makes a stock go up in value? The simple answer to that question is market demand. If more people are willing to pay more money for a stock, then the stock price ascends. It's commonly thought that higher sales and higher revenue are directly proportional to stock price, but this is not necessarily true. Companies don't need to have growing sales for the stocks to go up, but such growth is one of the signs that may demarcate a big winner.

The Price-to-Earnings Ratio

The P/E ratio allows you to evaluate how hot your penny stock is - at least in terms of its current ability to generate earnings. You have to be a bit wary here with penny stocks, as they can be seriously overvalued. To define the price-to-earnings ratio, divide the company's market cap by its earnings for the most recent year. You may also define the ratio by dividing the share price of the stock by the stock's revenue per share.

Let's go back to our example stock, Brayton Co. (BYT), which trades for $3 and has a market cap of $9 million. Now let's say that BYT's earnings for the past year were $6 million. BYT's price-to-earnings ratio would be 9/6 or 3/2. If you want to calculate its price-to-earnings ratio using earnings per share as the denominator, you simply divide the total revenue ($6 million) by the total number of outstanding shares ($3 million), and you have your earnings per share ($2). The BYT share price ($3) over earnings per share ($2) is 3/2.

Usually, as an investor, what you're looking for is a company that has a low price-to-earnings ratio. You want the company's per-share revenue to outstrip its per share cost. The only assumption you have to make is that more revenue leads to opportunities for more growth, and, of course, more growth means a higher stock valuation. A low price-to-earnings ratio can be another indicator that the stock is a good deal. In the case of BYT, it looks like its stock price is higher than its per share revenue, perhaps because its price-to-book ratio is favorable. Perhaps investors don't see an amazing growth opportunity but are willing to pay slightly more for the stock because its P/B ratio tells them its assets are intrinsically valuable.

Hopefully, you are beginning to see how various metrics connect with one another and can, in tandem, influence a stock's price along with its estimated growth potential. With penny stocks, the investor is faced simultaneously with both an advantage and a disadvantage.

The advantage is that, with good research and attention paid to key metrics, it's easier to spot promising penny stock investment opportunities, as penny stocks are more volatile in general. You're more likely to stumble upon a stock that's both cheap and has good growth potential.

The disadvantage, unfortunately, is related to the advantage. Because the stocks are so volatile and the financial reporting relatively more haphazard, many times, even the most well thought out plays don't have the desired result. You make money with penny stocks by continuing to make smart plays over a period of time and taking your losses with your wins.

When the Penny Stock Doesn't Have Earnings

Sometimes, what makes a penny stock a penny stock is the fact that its earnings are minimal or nonexistent. The stock could be taken to market well before the company posts a profit. When this happens, the P/E ratio is, of course, meaningless, because you have a zero in your denominator. Other ratios, such as the price-to-sales ratio and the price-to-cash-flow ratio, are incredibly important for these penny stocks. These ratios can be calculated in the same way as the price-to-revenue ratio; simply replace sales or cash flow data for revenue data. A good benchmark for a strong penny stock is when its share price is half the value of its per-share sales value. The cash flow metric is important to study if the company's earnings are questionable. Compare the price-to-cash flow and price-to-sales ratios for the company over several reporting periods to determine if they look coherent and are indicative of a healthy company. Then, if the price is right, make sure to buy.

Where Do I Find All These Ratios?

The ratios you use to evaluate penny stocks usually come directly from the exchange and are provided by your broker-dealer. Depending on the exchange, certain reporting practices are mandatory for companies that wish to have their stock traded on the exchange.

Chapter 11: Technical Analysis

When you make a plan to invest in penny stocks, you will most certainly need to know how and when to apply technical analysis, oftentimes referred to as TA ('Technical Analysis and Penny Stocks', 2019). The majority of skilled investors let their initial research on a stock revolve around the basics of technical analysis, so your goal should be to do the same. To do this successfully, however, you'll need to learn what technical analysis is and what practices, observations, and calculations it entails.

As an investor, your aim is to put your money into healthy and growing companies that employ knowledgeable workers, have positive profit margins, and of course, have a market share price that is gradually increasing. You can find all of this information by browsing through a company's annual reports - reports that all American companies and corporations are legally obligated to publish to the general public at the conclusion of each fiscal year. There are, of course, investors who prefer to predict the direction in which a company's share price will go by doing a simple review of the company's trading charts - and then they will apply TA. The shortcoming of this method, however, is that these investors tend to overlook the financial fundamentals of the company they are investing in.

When technical analysis is done correctly, investors

who complete TA have an advantage over the research forms other investors sometimes prefer to do. Unfortunately, this doesn't mean TA is a flawless economic approach. Like all things relating to finance and economics, you should always proceed with caution when you take on trading endeavors and opportunities. Oftentimes, a great cautionary approach to financial matters is to combine strategies. In other words, a cautious investor doesn't rely solely on TA, nor does he or she rely solely on the interpretation of a company's trading charts. Instead, a knowledgeable and cautious investor embraces TA and combines it with other approaches as well. It's recommended that you do initial research on a company of interest, applying TA to the current research you've completed, and then combining all of that information with full abstract and fundamental analysis review. This should give you all the vital financial information that you need to know about a company of interest.

The Positives of Technical Analysis

In this section, you'll discover the information and knowledge you need in order to become a more knowledgeable investor who is better prepared to succeed in the marketplace. The following list outlines highly effective and appropriate TA situations that you'll want to strive to meet:

- **Eliminate the required work for fundamental analysis.** Concerns regarding a company's growth, profit margins, and market shares can be eliminated when using TA. This is because you are not going to invest in a company - you are only trying to gain a profit from the share price.

- **Be a day trader, not a long-term one.** Many investment opportunities involve purchasing stocks from a healthy company in hopes of gaining a profit over an extended period of time and, as a result, an increase in the share price. If you can't wait around for the desired results, then TA is the quick fix for you.

- **Be informed about good buying and selling opportunities.** Pay attention to a company's chart patterns, changes in price directions, and trading volume. Technical analysis often shows very precise buy and sell points. To know when the best time to trade a penny stock is, you have to know how upward trends and drop-off in volumes work. We'll get to this a bit later.

- **Minimize investment exposure.** If you have any sort of investment, whether big or small, you're exposed. The best way to avoid exposure is to make trades in a short amount of time using TA techniques. Keep in mind, though, that while this shortens the time in which your money is exposed, it doesn't help eliminate the risk altogether.

- **Buy shares that trend in desirable price directions.** In other words, you're not buying shares in a specific company, per se. This makes the need to analyze a company's growth, interaction with competitors, and profit margins an unnecessary and altogether avoidable task.

- **Do the work.** If you decide to rely on TA, plan to make the interpretation of trading charts your new favorite hobby. Remember that many of the charts you'll encounter often don't highlight appropriate opportunities. With enough time, though, you'll come across charts (using TA) that show predictable patterns that you can further pursue - and by enough time, I mean about 20-40 hours a week spent in the open stock market.

- **Do what works best for you.** As a new or inexperienced investor, you'll need to spend time figuring out what tools work best for you, including TA. Feel free to use your personal preferences during financial endeavors.

- **It is possible to miss the really big gains.** Using TA means making smaller gains more often. Using this method might result in missing out on major percent moves and highly profitable opportunities. Don't be discouraged when this happens, as it will indeed happen.

> Success in penny stocks trading is achieved through patience and mental resilience.

If you find the points mentioned above appealing, then you'll probably find technical analysis equally appealing. However, there is no need to use TA and TA only in all of your investment decisions, but you can absolutely utilize it as a tool. Many investors who use TA to trade stocks avoid owning share overnight or during the weekend, because a lot can change when the market is closed, and those changes can impact the share prices once the market is open again. Take caution to that, because you cannot always react appropriately when events like that occur.

As detailed earlier, the best research approach involves using both a technical and fundamental review. With fundamental analysis, you can identify high-quality penny stocks that are moving in profitable directions. If you apply technical analysis to the trading charts of these stocks, you'll increase your ability to see and engage in highly rewarding buying and profit-making opportunities.

The Negatives of Technical Analysis

The more activity and trades involved in building a technical analysis pattern, the better. No matter the price dip or the resistance level, technical analysis will be more reliable. We can use political polls to demonstrate this. That is, not many people will invest if the results are based on the opinions of 50 people, but if the opinions are based on the polling of 1 million people, most will invest without hesitation. TA is no different; it's more reliable if the amount of the trading volume that generates the pattern is high. In other words, if the trading volume is low, the TA pattern won't appear to be so trustworthy.

Generally speaking, penny stocks have less trade activity than other stocks, which means some TA techniques simply can't be applied. This can be a major restriction at times. In addition to this drawback, some TA indicators can hint at a right price direction in the future, but sometimes this only applies when the underlying shares have been trading for a while. The effectiveness of TA depends on the situation and the stock, along with the factors listed below:

- **The percentage of shares trading hands.** If a single percent of total outstanding shares trade a day, the patterns that may form will most likely be unreliable. If a penny stock reveals a good indicator on 5 percent of shares every day, then this indicator can be considered highly reliable.

- **The daily trading volume.** Don't forget to watch the amount of shares trading hands every day. If you want to put your trust in technical analysis and the patterns it depicts, then you have to observe and understand the thousands of shares being bought and sold every day. The higher the number of shares, the more reliable the TA pattern will be.

Technical analysis with penny stocks is a very involving concept. Some TA patterns may work with some shares while other TA patterns may not. Every stock and every situation is very different from one another. The effectiveness of some financial indicators will vary from one penny stock to another. Like any other investment opportunity and endeavor, you will get better at it with time and practice.

Chapter 12: Working as a Professional

For every corporation that is traded publicly with the capitalization of the market in huge amounts of money, there are countless other small companies with market caps that are a lot more modest.

Since these companies don't have as big of operations or risks as others, they can be traded at much lower prices. I am talking, of course, about penny stocks. In this chapter, we will go over some of the dangers to stay aware of if you wish to become a penny stock pro.

Factors to Stay Aware of When Mastering Penny Stocks

Beware of the myth of the evolving stock, which is something that keeps people coming back time and time again to dabble with penny stocks is the assumption that the companies will grow and evolve into something huge and great. Although this is possible and happens at times, it isn't as common as proponents of penny stocks want you to think.

A lot of public firms choose to avoid going public until they have reached a big enough stance to make it worthwhile. Until this happens, they might opt for raising funds using corporate loans or private investors in addition to their typical operation methods. In general, these companies won't need IPOs initial public offerings) to fund their growth.

When companies offer their stock out at penny stock prices, it's typically due to one of these reasons: the company is on the verge of a huge expenditure and thinks that funds raised from an IPO could be the amount needed to finance this expenditure, or they have reached an apex in their size and want to disperse their earnings or shift the structure of their taxes.

In addition to those two reasons, there are some additional, less noble reasons that a company could opt for IPO when they aren't big yet. It could be because a company has been convinced that they should be involved with an IPO that's overhyped and overpriced by brokerage firms, hoping to make a quick buck by taking advantage of investors. It could also be the company owner's attempt to shift the ownership of the company over to others, as they don't see a bright future for the business.

It's a good idea to keep in mind that there is a huge range of companies within penny stocks and that the variance is immense. You could, for example, see a corporate structured company that specializes in prospecting oil right next to a farm that is family run and that specializes in crops.

Some businesses like these let investors chime in regarding who runs the show, while others are operations run by one person that falls apart when that person decides to retire. On average, bigger companies aim to please the people who invest in them, and companies using penny stocks don't always care about this aspect of the field.

How to Increase Your Effectiveness and Skill in Penny Stocks

A lot of great companies start off by trading with penny stocks, meaning that choosing to invest in these companies can pay off big time as they grow into larger stocks. But penny stocks don't typically have a positive name in the investment field, and, at times, this is for very good reasons. However, once you figure out a few methods for avoiding the negative possibilities of getting involved in penny stocks, you can find great companies that will pay off as fantastic rewards in the future.

Protection from the Downfalls of Investing in Penny Stocks

People who decide to invest but who don't learn about the most effective methods of protecting themselves from the risks that come along with penny stocks might end up getting burned. However, if you follow the points below, you will be able to avoid most scams, bad investments, and faulty information:

- Stick to higher caliber markets when possible - For the safest bets, try to stick with AMEX, NASDAQ, and OTCBB for your penny stock trading. While low caliber markets like OTC and the pink sheets can hold promise, it isn't worth the risk when you're first starting out.

- Do research and reach your own conclusions - Although well-meaning friends or family members might have a tip for you, you should never operate based on that alone. Remember to always do research on your own and reach an informed conclusion before investing to avoid losses and maximize your success with penny stocks.

- Stay away from free stock picks - Don't ever pursue these, no matter how alluring they may seem. When you hear about a stock through an email, a mailing list, or a free newsletter, they typically have some type of hidden motive. They'll try to trick people into buying stocks using tactics and false information, planning to get rid of the shares after convincing enough investors to trust them.

- Stick to solid stocks - You should only get involved with penny stocks that have solid fundamentals. If you aren't sure how to find this information, you can quickly look up the company online. Do a check for the position of their financial situation, and make a choice based on that.

- Be wary of story stocks - Watch out for stocks that come along with an incredible story. Very bad investments can have great business concepts, like the curing of a horrid disease or an engine design that will solve the pollution issues of our planet. However, stocks with fantastic stories such as these are most often bad companies in terms of finances, and the tempting nature of their concepts of business will have pushed their value way higher than it is in reality.

- Don't be afraid to call and ask - The more you know, the better. This means that calling the phone number for investor relations for the company you're looking into is a great idea. They should be more than happy to answer your questions, and knowing which ones to ask can allow you to discover quite easily how legitimate the business really is.

A Method for Getting Great at Investing in Penny Stocks

It's possible to practice your trading tactics in legitimate stocks in legitimate time, without risking any money. This is referred to as "paper trading" and involves using fake money for real stocks and learning by staying on top of how your picks do.

When you use this method, you can improve at investing in penny stocks quite quickly. Improving doesn't mean you have to risk actual money. As soon as you have reached a comfortable position in your investment knowledge and enjoy consistent profit with your fake trades, you can confidently switch to using real money. Here is how to do it:

1. Begin with a false amount of money - Keep an eye on the current, real penny stocks out there, and pick which one you would purchase with real capital.

2. Take notes - Start writing down the trades you would have made, including when you would buy and sell. Make sure to record the name of the stock, the date, the purchase's dollar amount, and the prices per share.

3. Invest in multiple - Do this with a lot of different penny stocks instead of only a couple, so you can get the most experience possible using this method. There is no reason to limit yourself to only one or two different practice stocks. The more you have, the better and faster you will learn.

4. Record which false investments were profitable

- Keep track of your success using fake money so you can figure out what methods of yours are successful and which you might be doing incorrectly. Write down your successful methods, so you know what to do more of and what to ease up on in the future.

If you make it a point to learn as much as possible about penny stocks through daily research in combination with trading with fake money using real stocks, you'll be well on your way to becoming a pro. It won't be long before you're ready to make the jump to real money and start earning profit.

Chapter 13: Don't Get Scammed

It's difficult not to consider a penny stock that's being advertised as the next big thing. Although it can easily be considered a scam, a lot of new investors still fall into this trap. There are thousands of publicly listed companies in a major stock exchange. However, so many individuals are still drawn to lesser-known penny stock companies ('How to Avoid Penny Stock Scams,' 2017).

A penny stock company listed on the Over-The-Counter Bulletin Board, an electronic system which shows real-time quotations, volume information, and last-sale prices of securities, is often advertised as being listed. On the other hand, a penny stock listed on the pink sheets isn't regulated by any financial organization or government entity. As such, it is a riskier investment than any other major stock company listed on a stock exchange. The company can post losses, and deficits can be huge. Furthermore, it can easily fold up. An investor can check with the Securities and Exchange Commission for information regarding a penny stock company.

Tools and Strategies Used In

Penny Stock Scams

Spam and junk mail can be distributed by scam artists to generate interest in a particular penny stock. In general, these emails contain fictitious information about the stock. It's highly advised to avoid buying the advertised stock just on the basis of any emails received. In addition, online bulletin boards are used to spread "hot tips" about a certain stock. Scammers use aliases to spread false information. Again, any interested investor must practice due diligence when they intend to invest in a penny stock. Some of these companies also pay stock promoters to offer "unbiased and independent" recommendations through the mass media. Before believing these paid promoters, it's best to investigate if they have financial certifications.

Cold calls and boiler room tactics are also used by fraudsters who have an organized group of high-pressure sales agents. These agents make cold calls to encourage potential investors to buy the penny stock. It's advised to be careful about receiving calls from unknown people. Furthermore, the penny stock company may issue dubious press releases. The potential investor must make it a point to investigate facts on his own so that he won't be scammed.

In case the individual is scammed, he can report the incident to his broker. If the latter doesn't resolve the issue, the former can report it to the Securities and

Exchange Commission or the securities regulator of the state.

Why People Become Interested in Penny Stocks

A penny stock offers the possibility to become rich quickly, which is exciting. It's the same concept as a lottery ticket, which offers a better future to the winner (if it's a winning ticket). An individual who invests in a penny stock is usually someone who doesn't perform mathematical computations to find out the penny stock company's intrinsic worth. He often is not one to analyze financial statements, industry studies, dividend projections, or discounted cash flows. In addition, a penny stock is like hidden knowledge; an investor who has an interest in a certain stock often feels special, because he knows something that the others don't know. If he talks about his investment, people will listen, because it is something they haven't heard about.

A penny stock lacks liquidity. This is why a lot of experts don't recommend buying this kind of stock. However, it is also very volatile, meaning that the price may experience wild fluctuations, creating a lot of opportunities to profit quickly. An inexperienced investor may continuously buy shares of the penny stock because the price continuously goes up. He doesn't realize that he is one of the people who drive up the price. In case he intends to sell his shares, he soon realizes that no one wants to buy the stock anymore. An investor decides to invest in a certain penny stock because he believes that this company is the next Microsoft or Walmart. He fails to recognize that these companies, which started from humble beginnings, offered shares to the public when they have grown large already. These companies opted for IPOs due to their desire to expand the business.

Actually, these investing traps can be avoided if the investor thinks of himself as the owner of the penny stock company. He has to take his emotions out from the investment equation in order to make a realistic and correct decision. Liquidity isn't even a problem if the penny stock company continues to grow.

Considerations in Buying a Penny Stock

A lot of traditional investors have become rich due to having invested in high-quality stocks; but only a few, if any, have become rich from penny stock investing. The power of compounding consistent gains from high-quality stocks is the single factor responsible for the enormous wealth of these traditional investors. Their chosen companies continuously increase their profits and offer high returns for the investors' money.

Dividends are often distributed to shareholders, and investors continuously buy shares to increase their earnings.

On the other hand, an investor in a penny stock company can't increase his shares because of liquidity problems. If he continues to buy, he will cause the price of the share to increase. The penny stock is inefficient; therefore, an investor has to buy at higher costs for every transaction. These costs reduce any profit that may be earned from his investment. In fact, he may even lose money because of these frictional costs.

Types of Penny Stock Scams

Inexperienced investors often fall into the hands of penny stock scammers deceiving them to invest in cheap and worthless stock. Most of the time, traders lose money after investing in such scams. As a beginner, you need to be aware of all these scams, which are detailed below (Reynolds, 2018).

Reverse merger - At times, a private company will collaborate with a public company for them to be a publicly traded firm not having to pass through the stress of a more traditional method. This kind of step results in the company changing its earnings and inflating the prices of its stock. Though, we do have some legitimate reverse mergers; determining a genuine one can be done simply by reviewing the business' history and picking out speckled activities in its merger

Pump-and-dump schemes - There is a common scam where stock promoters oftentimes get investors' interest in an unknown stock, leading the novice to buy the shares. Then, the moment the stock gets to a given inflated price, the fraudsters will sell off shares, thereby dumping the stock at huge profits. With this act, traders end up in a high and dry situation. Often, this strategy is spread via free penny stock newsletters in which the publishers have been paid to include overrated and unpromising stocks. In case you come across any of such newsletters, get more details on their site and get to know the initiator.

Short-and-distort - This scam is used to make profits. Shorting works when stocks are borrowed by investors and then sold immediately in an open market at a higher price, anticipating that the company's stock will fall; by then, though, they can scoop up the shares they have sold at a lesser price. After this, they give these borrowed shares back to the owners. Some frauds of penny stock usually short-sell a stock and see that there's a fall in the stock by the dissemination of rumors that are untrue about the company. Short sellers make a lot from their fraudulent strategy, while investors end up on the losing side.

Guru scam - There are several fake ads, and unfortunately, people fall victim to them easily. Often, these ads will talk about ways they became successful by using a special secret to eventually earn enough for things such as lakefront houses, glitzy, boats, and cars, etc. For a small amount, these so-called "experts" will promise to share their secret with you. Please make sure you trash any email you receive from someone promising to make you rich.

Avoiding Scams

There is so much manipulation in the penny stock market, including fraud and chicanery. There is then a need for investors to know that this kind of act is not the dominant situation of micro-caps and penny stocks. Is there a way for a serious trader to avoid getting into the hands of fraudulent penny stock promoters? Take a look below at some suggestions that might help you.

Determine the credibility of the company - The success of any organization depends solely on the leadership, and this is also true for penny stock companies. You will never see a top-rated manager in charge of a penny stock company. Moreover, you should go through the track record of the management to review successes or failures of the directors and executives and also to see if there exists any general issues or legal issues.

Differentiate between research and promotion

- Promoters often employ writers of newsletters to formulate a dishonest story about their stock. They mostly come up with a compelling story for investors in penny stock through the use of outlandish projections, hyperbole, and in some scenarios, a deliberate misrepresentation. As a penny stock trader, you must be able to differentiate between stock promotion and true equity research. You will be able to conclude if it's an advertisement by finding out if the writer was paid to write when you read the "disclosures" section.

Quality of dischosure - A company that provides more disclosure is an indication of its high level of corporate transparency. By investing in a company that you know little or nothing about or in stock that you are advised by the OTC to be careful of, you are putting yourself in a danger zone. A penny stock company that has been involved in suspicious promotional activities like spam emails or ones that have a case of fraudulent activity at hand could earn this kind of stigma.

Chapter 14: Tips and Tricks

Penny stock trading is a risky venture, but with the right information in hand and good guidance, you should be able to avoid the risks and dance around the manholes that litter the road to penny stock success.

Here are some tips that can help you to avoid falling into a schemer's trap and ensure that you receive a good profit in every transaction:

- Refrain from believing stories. The world of penny stock trading and investment is full of people whose main goal is to lure unwitting investors to fall into their deceitful scams and schemes. One way of doing so is by spreading stories across the internet that tell of individuals who made it big in penny stocks by doing this and that or visiting sites here and there. Most of the time, these stories are sent through emails and posted on social networking sites, which are platforms that can reach a lot of people efficiently in a short period of time. If ever you encounter these stories in your email or in forums, it's best to ignore them.

- Focus on good penny stocks only. It is recommended that you put your focus in penny stocks that will surely give you profits. Look at how the stock's earnings grow. Make sure that they are consistent and make 52-week highs. They should also have good earnings breakout and trade in volumes of at least 100,000 shares.

- Lengthen your search time. Stocks that consistently appear in the listings of exchanges are more likely to be consistent performers also. This will help you avoid falling for stocks with only short bursts of luck.

- Pay no heed to tips. Like stories, tips on penny stocks abound the internet. Mostly, these tips are about when to sell and what penny stocks to sell, and they're usually delivered to people through their emails or distributed through penny stock newsletters.

- Always look for disclaimers. In connection with the previous paragraph, one way to avoid getting fooled by tips is to look at the disclaimer portion of the newsletter that contained the tip. There's actually nothing wrong with penny stock newsletters by themselves. In fact, they can serve as ways for small, growing companies to gain publicity. The problem with them is that newsletter publishers are paid to give these tips and spotlight a company's stock. However, most of the time, they also print good information about how a company is doing despite their very poor performance. To avoid getting fooled, you should read the disclaimers that are printed in the newsletters, which are usually found in the bottom section. Disclaimers are required by the Securities Exchange Commission to be included in newsletters, and it's there that the real purpose of the tip is indicated.

- Get your hands off of fast-growing stocks quickly. For an investor who has just started trading in penny stocks, getting your hands on stocks with a large and fast growth that can reach around 25 percent is absolutely amazing. Usually, beginners tend to be amazed too much and want to reach a higher return. However, veteran penny stock traders recommend letting go of these kinds of stocks quickly. For one reason, you should grab the chance of benefiting from the stock when it's at its highest performance. Another reason is that stocks with good performance within only just days are more likely to have been subjected to the pumping and dumping scheme.

- There are sources that say that shorting penny stocks is a good way to earn more profit. However, shorting penny stocks is best left to the more experienced and professional penny stocks traders and investors. The problem with penny stock shorting is that penny stocks are unpredictable, which can lead you to lose large sums of money instead of gaining profit. Another point is that it's quite hard to look for penny stocks to short.

- Know what stocks to buy. Buying the wrong kinds of stocks will not help you gain any profit, but will bring you loss instead. Experts recommend buying stocks which trade equal to, or more than, 100,000 shares per day. Investing in shares that trade in high volumes will make things easier for you when you want to get them off your hands. The importance of research again enters the picture here. You must know the volume of the shares traded and the volume of the dollars.

- Avoid trading big. Although you need to invest in stocks that trade in high volume for each day, you should also avoid trading at least 10 percent of that stock's daily trading volume. For example, for a stock that trades 100,000 share volumes, you can buy 10,000 shares.

There is a large number of outright lies and misleading information out there concerning penny stocks. Now that you have invested your time into learning how to be successful in penny stock investments, below are some helpful tips to remember as you venture forward into successfully becoming financially free by wisely trading in penny stocks:

Invest in your education - It can be easy to get overly confident when you have a few good trades under your belt, especially if you're new at trading in penny stocks. You won't ever really know it all, and that's why it's so important to make the furthering of your penny stock education such a high priority. It can also be very beneficial for you to seek out the investors who you think have achieved what you would like to achieve in penny stocks and then learn everything you possibly can from them. If you are lucky, you will get in contact with a seasoned penny stock trader who will share their knowledge and findings with you and help you to become a stronger and more informed trader.

Remember that only about 5-10 percent of investors out there consistently make a profit. It also may be a good idea just to ignore what traders happen to say in chat rooms, on message boards, and on the trader social networks. Most traders will tell you that they are making consistent, good money with the sole purpose of trying to sell you something. This is extremely common when it comes to penny stocks, which means that it would be a good idea for you to choose your mentor(s) wisely. One way to identify a legitimate mentor is by seeing if they are completely transparent. Ask for your mentor's records of trades, as well as tax statements showing their profits. If that mentor hesitates or retreats, so should you.

Use a journal to keep track of your trades - As a beginning penny stock investor, it would be in your best interest to start a trading journal that includes the moves you have made, which size positions that you decided to take, and if you had a profit or loss on that trade. Your trade diary will end up teaching you a lot about trading and about yourself as an investor. This simple but valuable resource will help you to become consistently profitable. The most successful traders around are very methodical; they don't make plays on just a whim. Successful traders take their past actions into consideration and then utilize their experiences in order to better their odds at making successful trades in the future. The information concerning the trades you have made in the past will be extremely useful when honing your skills as a penny stock trader.

Give back to your community - Just like anyone else, traders tend to get caught up in the day to day activities. Traders bury themselves in their work, and it can be difficult to pay attention to anything that isn't making them money after a while. That is just not what life's about, though. Make the time to get some of your hard-earned money together, and use that money to impact just one family in your community. It can be really humbling to see someone gushing over simple, inexpensive new clothes, a washing machine, or a gift card for a grocery store. This will change your view of money. There is nothing like it in the entire world.

Have respect for risk - You should respect the fact that risk is a huge (if not the biggest) part of trading penny stocks. Things can change very quickly when trading penny stocks. A penny stock that you may think is on the rise can actually go south in mere moments, and vice versa. One of the biggest reasons that penny stocks are so risky is because most of the companies that issue them do not meet the SEC filing requirements. Actually, the bottom line here is that you simply do not know what you may be in for with penny stocks. The risk in penny stocks is inherent. You may not be able to fight it, but you can make a choice to respect it. Make sure that the position you take is not big enough to affect the stock's price.

Don't believe everything you hear - In fact, you should rarely believe what you hear about penny stocks. By this point in the book, that statement should sound pretty redundant. People who promote penny stocks are really quick to try and sell you grandiose stories about extremely exciting companies that are about to blow up and forever change our world with their magical new products. These are, of course, lies and hype. Penny stock companies are not usually legitimate companies; if they were legitimate companies, they would be traded on the AMEX or the NYSE and not priced like common lottery tickets. In all actuality, about 99 percent of every penny stock company will ultimately fail, so the odds of you catching the mere 1 percent that does grow is very slim. Do not believe all that you hear about penny stock trading, and discover the truth for yourself. Those companies may all be scammers, schemers, and thieves, but that does not necessarily mean that you can't use them right back in order to make a profit.

Adjust your profit expectations - Another huge piece of hype that you will often encounter with penny stock promoters is about how fast your investment will grow. While it's possible for a penny stock to go from $1 per share to $10 per share, it is unrealistic to try to make more than about $0.75. Don't get greedy. It's great if you make more than that, but keep in mind that by keeping your trades small, you are keeping your losses small, as well. Practicing this will result in you making a lot of money in the long run. If you're always going after big wins, you will end up forcing trades that really aren't there. This is the type of mistake that will push you out of the game before you ever get a chance to play.

Take care of yourself - Finally, make sure you are taking care of yourself while you're working so hard at finding financial freedom. It's really easy to get so wrapped up in stocks and trading that you forget to take care of yourself. This is very easy to let happen. Keep in mind that you really have nothing if not your health. It can be difficult to remember to eat a healthy meal and get some exercise when you are so busy watching charts all day long and then researching all night, but it is so very important. You will end up being a much better trader if you're in good health, and you will also be able to live longer and enjoy more of the benefits of your success if you take good care of yourself. Get rid of the bad habits now before you're set in a bad stock routine. Focus on staying healthy, so your good health is there to support you all throughout your long, successful career.

Chapter 15: How to Find the Right Help

If it's hard to find good help these days, then it's exceptionally hard to find good help and advice in the world of stock trading - and it's excruciatingly difficult to find good help with penny stock investing. The main problem is that the massive clutter of nonsense and scammers makes getting sound advice like finding a needle in a haystack. In this chapter, you'll learn some tricks to locate credible sources of advice as you pursue your fortune in penny stock investing.

Screen Your Advice and Advisors

Penny stock investors must have screening criteria. Otherwise, the sheer quantity of penny stocks on the market may baffle you; you simply can't research them all. The challenge lies in the presence of many individuals who want to offer advice and, unfortunately, not all of them have your best interest at heart. Here are some indicators that you can look for when you're wondering whether a stock advisor, TV personality, broker, or some combination of all of the above has your best interests at heart.

The media superstar - Stock experts are often seeking fame and an audience. While being able to muster up good stock picks can definitely help an expert gain credibility, there are sometimes other attributes that factor into whether a stockbroker eventually appears on television, such as that person's charisma, sense of humor, and all around personality. If you want to check a TV personality's actual competency as an investment advisor, investigate their track record. Have the stocks the advisor has recommended performed well over time, or are they in the position they're in merely because they're sure to draw good ratings?

The fragile ego - Some investment advisors hate being wrong and continue to insist that a stock is undervalued for years on end, regardless of the evidence. Spot these personalities, and learn how to distinguish between what may actually be sound advice and what's merely the product of the advisor's insistence on his own infallibility.

The sociopath - There is a particular class of investors who are unsettlingly common on the penny stock scene that don't really care at all about whether or not the advice they provide is legitimate, profitable, or even based in reality. They believe that stocks exist in an essentially chaotic universe, and the only role of the broker is to encourage transactions and collect commissions. These individuals often don't even enjoy their jobs. They are chronically difficult to reach, reluctant to provide information, and quick to pull the authority card, wanting you to trust them for no reason other than that they're the purported "experts."

Look for a Verifiable Track Record

Brokers, advisors, or other stock experts who are serious about supplying good advice are proud of what they've accomplished for their clients. They want to show you their statistics and proven ability to read the market.

In the penny stock world, these brokers and advisors stand out, because it's easy to contact and communicate with them. They don't hide behind a shadowy brand that changes every year after the company ruins its reputation by giving out bad advice.

You want to see a track record that spans at least a year, if not substantially longer. Spend some time verifying that the picks and successes reported are accurate and not just made up. One way to verify the accuracy of an advisor's pick sheet is to follow his picks for a time and then check to make sure that the picks he made are the same as those reported on his track record.

Skepticism is good, but at some point, you're going to have to trust someone, or you're not going to go anywhere. Always be ready to establish the difference between the two archetypes of a bad stock analyst and a good one who's on a bit of a cold streak. At some point, it's just going to come down to trust; you must trust the person who's helping you invest your money. Your challenge is to cultivate trust with someone based on a series of rational evaluation points, including criteria that go beyond how well a person dresses, his golf score, or his political affiliation.

Conclusion

You should now have the foundational knowledge needed to enter the world of penny stock trading. The lessons that you've learned in this book can only be used to the greatest effect when you set time and be patient about making intelligent trades based on what you've learned. Regardless of the trading style that you adopt, whether that is day trading or value trading, you must be aware of the total trading volume and liquidity for every company that you invest in. To be a successful day trader, you need to dedicate an entire day to trading, making at least four bets in a single day. If you go down this path, you will be relying on pattern recognition, volatility, and strong liquidity to earn you a steady and consistent profit.

If you decide that you're more tuned to value trading, then you know that you'll be relying on research and investing in companies that have either an underlying patent or asset that isn't reflected in their market cap. In addition to these details, you will need suitable liquidity to sell stock once the price has been adjusted. How you research and find the valuable assets of these smaller companies is going to depend on the sector you are most interested in researching.

Stick with what you know; if you work in technology, focus on penny stocks related to tech. If you work in any specific sector of the economy, focus on companies with backgrounds that you can understand

and fit into the grander economy. It's not that you are waiting for these companies to suddenly make millions, but rather, you will understand their underlying assets and know when the market capitalization does not accurately reflect the value of the company.

Regardless of the trading strategy that you decide to invoke, please make a trade log and use it diligently. It's also recommended that you use this trade log to do one week of fake trading - that is, one week where you make trades and log them in your notebook. Use this practice week and focus on why you chose the stocks that you did. Also, try to determine what mistakes, if any, you have made. For day traders, mistakes commonly come down to improperly predicting market liquidity (not able to sell their holdings). For value traders, a common mistake is overvaluing an asset. Make sure that you have a proper assessment of a company if you believe their holdings are above their market capitalization. Both strategies require practice, and you will get better with this in time.

If you enjoyed this book or received value from it in any way, then I'd like to ask you for a favor: would you be kind enough to leave a review for this book on Amazon? It'd be greatly appreciated!

References

Basenese, L. (2017). Decoding the Cryptic "Pink Sheets." Retrieved from https://www.wallstreetdaily.com/2017/05/15/decoding-cryptic-pink-sheets/

Beers, B. (2018). Introducing pink sheets: the OTC market. Retrieved from https://www.investopedia.com/articles/fundamental-analysis/08/pink-sheets-ottcb.asp

Hayes, A. (2013). Stocks Basics: What Are Stocks?. Retrieved from https://www.investopedia.com/university/stocks/stocks1.asp

How To Avoid Penny Stock Scams | MyPennyStocksHub.com. (2017). *MyPennyStocksHub.com.* Retrieved 9 May 2019, from https://mypennystockshub.com/avoid-penny-stock-scams/

Leeds, P. (2019). 6 Proven Financial Ratios Reveal Winning Penny Stocks. Retrieved from https://www.thebalance.com/penny-stock-proven-ratios-2637035

Leeds, P. (2019). The Best Investors Share These 6 Personality Traits. Retrieved from https://www.thebalance.com/investor-personality-traits-3867158

Lewis, M. (2019). How to Pick and Trade Penny Stocks. Retrieved from https://www.wikihow.com/Pick-and-Trade-Penny-Stocks

LIOUDIS, N. (2019). The Difference Between Stock Trades on Pink Sheets and the OTCBB. Retrieved from https://www.investopedia.com/ask/answers/what-does-it-mean-when-stock-trades-pink-sheets-or-otcbb/

Metcalf, T. (2019). Why Do Companies Sell Stocks?. Retrieved from https://smallbusiness.chron.com/companies-sell-stocks-59896.html

Murphy, C. (2018). How to invest in penny stocks for beginners. Retrieved from https://www.investopedia.com/articles/investing/091114/how-invest-penny-stocks.asp

MURPHY, C. (2019). A Review of Pink Sheet Stocks and How Investors Can Trade Them. Retrieved from https://www.investopedia.com/terms/p/pinksheets.asp

Murphy, C. (2019). How to Find and Invest in Penny Stocks (ADAT, ANAD). Retrieved from https://www.investopedia.com/updates/how-to-invest-in-penny-stocks/

Murphy, C. (2019). How to Find and Invest in Penny Stocks (ADAT, ANAD). Retrieved from https://www.investopedia.com/updates/how-to-invest-in-penny-stocks/

Reynolds, C. (2018). Entrepreneurs, Be Careful to Avoid Penny Stock Scams | The Startup Magazine. Retrieved from http://thestartupmag.com/common-penny-stock-scams-look/

Staff, M. (2016). *What Is a Penny Stock? -- The Motley Fool. The Motley Fool.* Retrieved 8 May 2019, from https://www.fool.com/knowledge-center/what-is-a-penny-stock.aspx

Technical Analysis and Penny Stocks. (2019). *Extraordinaryinvestor.com.* Retrieved 9 May 2019, from https://www.extraordinaryinvestor.com/technical-analysis.html

Trading Strategy. (2019). *Investopedia.* Retrieved 9 May 2019, from https://www.investopedia.com/trading-strategy-4427764

What are Penny Stocks and How Do They Work? - Wall Street Survivor. (2019). *Wall Street Survivor.* Retrieved 9 May 2019, from https://www.wallstreetsurvivor.com/starter-guides/what-are-penny-stocks-how-they-work/

Made in the USA
Middletown, DE
11 July 2019